THE LAST LEAF ON THE TREE

how to make the **MOST** *of the* **REST** *of your* **LIFE**

TEXAS BAPTIST MISSIONS FOUNDATION

Paul W. Powell

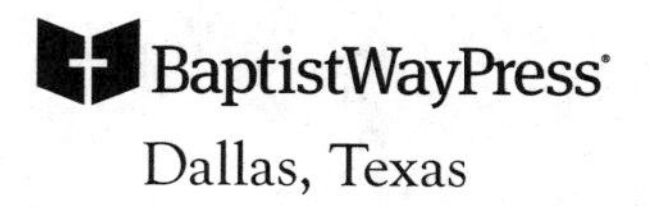

Dallas, Texas

The Last Leaf on the Tree: How to Make the Most of the Rest of Your Life

This book was produced in cooperation with the
Texas Baptist Missions Foundation.
Bill Arnold, President.

BAPTISTWAY PRESS® Leadership Team
Executive Director, Baptist General Convention of Texas: David Hardage
Director, Great Commission Team: Delvin Atchison
Publisher, BaptistWay Press®: Scott Stevens

Cover Design: Lindsay Galvin
Interior Design and Production: Desktop Miracles, Inc.
Printing: Data Reproductions Corporation

First edition: April 2016
ISBN-13: 978-1-938355-59-2

Doris Jones Lane
Gloria Ortega
Joyce Milburn
Three great secretaries who carried me in my Tyler years longer than Moses carried the children of Israel in the Wilderness.

A BRIEF HISTORY OF THE
Texas Baptist Missions Foundation

Begun as a two-year experiment to raise additional funds for new churches, the Texas Baptist Missions Foundation has, for the past thirty years, worked with generous Baptists to support mission activities in Texas and around the world. The mission statement of the Foundation is simple:

> To the glory of God, develop innovative partnerships with followers of Christ who want to use their resources to change the world.

With that statement as the guideline, the Foundation has worked with over 33,000 different donors to support more than 250 different mission projects all over Texas and around the world. Because the Foundation is supported by the Texas Baptist Cooperative Program, every dollar of the funds given though the Foundation is used for its intended purpose. The Foundation provides $1.00 of mission money for every 13 cents of Cooperative Program money that it receives.

Working with donors and forming innovative partnerships is an exciting challenge. Those partnerships have included providing funds to build operating rooms for a Baptist hospital in Mexico, developing a no-interest loan program for low-income churches, helping start more than twelve hundred new churches, building and equipping a tool trailer for the Texas Baptist Men retiree builders, building a community center in Japan, and building four Baptist Student Ministry buildings on college campuses—just to name a few.

The ways that donors funded these projects are as varied as the projects themselves. Many were funded by gifts of cash or stocks and bonds. For others, a charitable trust that provided income to the donor and spouse was the best method of achieving their goals. Sometimes there were gifts of a tangible asset—like land—that provided the needed resources.

"To the glory of God" is an important part of the Foundation's mission statement. That is the reason the Foundation exists and the goal of every visit with a donor and the goal of every partnership that receives funds. It is a great joy for the staff to work with people who want to make a difference in Texas and around the world, and to do it to God's glory.

The Texas Baptist Missions Foundation is a part of the Baptist General Convention of Texas.

May We Help You?

If you would like to explore ways you can make a difference for God's kingdom with a portion of your resources, the Missions Foundation can help. No matter the size of your gift, the Foundation staff is willing to help you use it in whatever way you feel the Lord leading. Whether by making a gift of cash or other asset, establishing a trust, or giving something through your will, we can assist you in selecting the best method for you to accomplish your giving goal. If you would like to explore the possibilities, give us a call at (800)558–8263 or visit our website www.texasbaptists.org/tbmf.

The Last Leaf on the Tree

Table of Contents

Introduction

Near his eighty-seventh birthday, President Harry S. Truman, who had been hospitalized with pneumonia, went to recuperate in St. Petersburg, Florida. All of his contemporaries were dead, including politician Adlai Stevenson, Prime Minister Winston Churchill, and General Douglas McArthur. When word came of the death of President Dwight Eisenhower, his biographer described Truman as "beginning to feel like the last leaf on the tree."[1]

I think I know how he felt. Almost all of my high school buddies, my college roommates, and the friends I worked closely with during sixty years of ministry are now gone—including James Landes, Herb Reynolds, John Baugh, Paul Piper, Charles McLaughlin, Milton Cunningham, Hershel Hobbs, Winfred Moore, and countless others. Since I started this book, I can add Lester Collins and Phil Lineberger to the list. In moments of nostalgia, I feel both joy and sadness.

On one hand, I am glad I've hung on such a long time. There is some virtue in not dropping off or being blown away by the winds of time and change. While attending seminary I carpooled from Bell County with several other student pastors. They were all super smart, going far beyond me to earn their doctorates and teach in universities or become denominational leaders. Unbeknownst to me until recently, they were talking in my absence one day and deemed me the least likely in the group to stay in the ministry. But after sixty years in the ministry, I'm still hanging on. That's worth something.

I've also had the joy of being a part of a team—something bigger than myself. One leaf does not make a tree. Leaves have to be attached—first to branches, then to a trunk that is rooted in the earth. Likewise, I stayed attached to my church, and my church stayed attached to an association. My association stayed attached to a state convention and my state to a national convention, and my convention was rooted deep in historical and biblical soil. Together, we had staying power. I am privileged to have been associated with and work alongside some great people who accepted me, encouraged me, and let me be a part of something bigger and more lasting than myself.

I have a beautiful oak tree in my yard with big, broad leaves. Every fall the leaves turn brown, but they don't turn loose from the branches. I marvel that while the other trees are bleak and barren throughout winter, this oak remains fully leaved. They stay there until the springtime when new growth finally pushes them off and replaces them. I've watched that tree carefully this spring. It's May and there are still about five old leaves hanging on. But soon a strong wind will come and they'll be gone.

That's the cycle of life. As I took the place of those before me, others will gently shove me aside and take my place one day. I'm okay with that. As has been said, "The workman dies, but the work goes on." Our labor is not in vain.

It's been good to hang around so long and be a part of so many good things. For all of that, "Thanks be to God the father and our Lord Jesus Christ" . . . and to you, friends.

PAUL POWELL
TYLER, TEXAS
2015

NOTES

1. David McCullough, *Truman* (New York, NY: Simon & Schuster, 1993), 86.

The longer we live, the harder it is to keep our balance—not just physically, but also spiritually. Keeping our spiritual balance is one key to a full life.

1

Keep Your Balance

Psalm 39:4–7

Whenever I go to my doctor, his nurse asks me, "Have you fallen lately?" My standard reply is, "Of course I have." That's what old people do. We fall around. I haven't fallen lately, but if it weren't for walls, door facings, and handrails, I'd be falling all over the place. When people get older, they lose their sense of balance, their equilibrium gets off, and their steps aren't as steady as they once were.

Today when my pastor and I do a funeral together, I tell him to go down the steps first so that I can put my hand on his shoulder and brace myself. In the Scriptures, Jesus told Peter that very thing would happen to him. He said, "I tell you the truth, when you were younger you dressed yourself and went where you wanted; but when you are old you will stretch out your hands, and someone else will dress you and lead you where you do not want to go" (John 21:18). Now that's happened to me.

Balance is important in all of life. A football team needs to have a balanced attack that includes running as well as passing. Otherwise the defense can key in on one aspect of the game. A basketball team needs to have balance in scoring so that the opposition can't double-team its best player. The famed coach John Wooden pointed out that no team with the leading scorer in the nation ever won the national championship. The reason? You only have to stop one man to win the game.

We also need balance in our finances. There's an old saying, "If your outgo exceeds your income, your upkeep will be your downfall."

Balance is important, not just in sports and finances, but also in every aspect of our spiritual lives. We need it there for the same reason we need it in every other area: so we won't fall. For example, the Bible teaches that we need a balance in our Christian life between faith and works. Psalm 39 tells about a man who was about to lose his spiritual footing. He had lost his balance spiritually and was on the verge of falling into sin. We're not sure what his problem was. It could have been sickness or emotional distress. Perhaps someone had wronged him. Nothing can throw us off balance like going through difficulty. Hard times are hard on faith.

His first reaction to his situation was anger. He was tempted to lash out with harsh words at or about God. But as he considered his options, he thought better of it and held his tongue. Instead of complaining, he started praying. That's always a better alternative.

First, he asked the Lord to help him realize that we are weak, frail creatures. He wanted to understand how brief his days were and to appreciate what little time he had left. Life at its best is a short span, a vapor. He also saw how temporary our possessions are and how futile it is to trust in wealth – hurrying and worrying, fretting and sweating, accumulating things that will all be left behind for someone else. Finally, he realized and affirmed that his hope and ultimate security was in the Lord. The Lord was not his problem. He was his hope.

This is how he says it in Psalm 39:

> Show me, O LORD, my life's end and the number of my days; let me know how fleeting is my life. You have made my days a mere handbreadth; the span of my years is as nothing before you. Each man's life is but a breath. 'Selah' Man is a mere phantom as he goes to and fro: He bustles about, but only in vain; he heaps up wealth, not knowing who will get it. But now, Lord, what do I look for? My hope is in you (Ps. 39:4–7).

In his struggles and through his reflection, the psalmist realized three principles to help him keep his spiritual balance. If you know these truths, they will also help keep you on your feet. When the pressures of life mount, they will steady you if you remember:

- No matter how long we live, life is short.
- No matter how much we accumulate, we leave it all behind.
- No matter how dark the night, we are never without hope.

We Are All Lingering

First, no matter how long we live, life is short. Only as we look at life from the vantage point of death can we keep our spiritual balance. The thrust of the opening lines of the psalmist's prayer was for the Lord to help him know how fragile we are, how brief our days are, and how transient life is. In fact, he describes his days as a handbreadth and a vapor.

A handbreadth was an ancient unit of measurement. In the days before rulers, people used the width of the human hand as one of the smallest and most convenient measurements. Three hands would make a foot; nine hands would make a yard. It was not exact, but it was close enough in the early days of crude building.

The psalmist saw his life as that small measurement—a narrow span, a mere breath. This echoes the words of James, who asks, "What is your life?" To that, he answers, "You are a mist that appears for a little while and then vanishes"

(James 4:14). When you venture outside on a cool day and exhale, your warm breath meets the cold air and forms a vapor. Stand there just a moment and it will vanish completely. That's a picture of your life and mine. In the sight of God, our years are just a moment. Realizing the brevity of our time on earth will help us maintain our balance and keep things in perspective.

It's a short step between reading obituaries and needing one yourself. When Emily Phillips was diagnosed at age 69 with pancreatic cancer, she knew she did not have long to live. So she decided to give the world a farewell in her own words and penned her own obituary. Many can relate to what she wrote about the brevity of life, which read in part, "So . . . I was born; I blinked; and it was over."[1]

Several years ago a CBS mini-series entitled *Comanche Moon* told the story of two Texas Rangers battling Native Americans on the plains of Texas. The two main characters, Gus and Captain Woodrow, were talking one day about Gus' wife who had died after a prolonged illness. As Gus shared how she suffered, his friend (who had never married) clearly didn't understand this kind of grief. In Woodrow's mind, when someone was that sick there was no need to linger. However, Gus' astute observation was that "we are all just lingering." That's what the Scriptures are saying to us.

Our average life expectancy keeps getting longer and longer. When I was born in 1933, my average life expectancy was 61.7 years. Today it is 78.8. That's a healthy increase. But no matter how much the number increases, it will never be enough. No matter how long we live, we realize as we look back how brief our days have been, and we wonder where the time went. Justice Oliver Wendell Holmes, Jr., when he approached the age of ninety, is said to have told American statesman Dean Acheson, "If the ceiling should open and through the opening should come the voice of God saying, 'Wendell, you have five minutes to live,' I should reply, 'Very well, Boss, but I wish it were ten.'"

I understand how he felt. In 2001 at the age of sixty-seven, I was having a routine stress test when my doctor suddenly shut off the treadmill. I was surprised since I felt okay and told him I could go a little longer.

He replied, "No, I don't like what I see. We need to give you an arteriogram immediately."

The arteriogram revealed I had blockages. One vessel was 50% blocked, three were 70–75% blocked, and six were 80–95% blocked. I was a walking time bomb. I had never had a heart attack, but my plumbing was completely clogged up. When the surgeon saw my test results, he concluded I would require seven bypasses. I asked him to do eight so I could make it into the Guinness Book of World Records, but apparently seven is the maximum number possible!

The surgery went without a hitch. When the doctor visited me in my hospital room the next day, he told me he thought he'd bought me ten more years.

I responded, "I'll settle for that," figuring that would carry me to seventy-seven, the average life span for a man at that time.

But I didn't realize how quickly ten years would pass. So on the tenth anniversary of my surgery, I wrote to my doctor, "I have made my ten years. Now I either want a new contract or a new doctor."

By then I had lived the average life span, but it wasn't nearly enough. I wanted more time.

In 2015 Dr. Ezekiel Immanuel, a bioethicist and one of the main architects of Obamacare, suggested that people over age seventy-five should stop having annual checkups. This, he proposed, would be a way to control the high cost of medical care for the elderly and make The Affordable Care Act affordable. His logic was that a huge part of health care costs are spent on the last few years of our lives—some say more than all the rest of life put together. The implication seemed to be that people over eighty lose their vitality and creative mojo and can no longer contribute to work, society, or to the world. It would be better for us to go on and get out of the way. He then was so bold as to say he wanted to die at seventy-five. I want to say two things about that. One, I would be happy for Ezekiel Immanuel to die at seventy-five. And second, when he is seventy-four I'd like to ask him how he feels about it. When he made that rash statement, he was only fifty-eight years of age. My hunch is that he will have changed his mind by then and want more time. Most everyone does.

The Scriptures say, "Teach us to number our days aright that we may gain a heart of wisdom" (Ps. 90:12). If you had one day to live, what friends and family would you call or write? What would you say? What things left undone would you do? Do them now, today, while you can. Time is fleeting, so we should take time to enjoy the little things. One day we may realize they were really the *big* things. Live so that you have no regrets. Express your love to your family and friends, and give God his rightful place in your life.

Life's a journey to eternity, and at the end of the road is God. Walk faithfully after him, and you'll be able to keep your balance. Remember to do it now because life is brief, so very brief.

Not What We Gather but What We Scatter Matters

The second principle that will help you stay balanced is the realization that no matter how much you accumulate, you will leave it all behind. To live a balanced life we need not only a proper perspective of time but also a proper perspective of things. So the psalmist says, "He bustles about, but only in vain; he heaps up wealth, not knowing who will get it" (Ps. 39:6). We hurry and worry, fret and sweat to have more and more, and we'll leave it all behind for someone else.

Jesus told a parable that illustrates this very truth. He told about a rich man's farm that was very productive, so productive in fact that he had no place to store all that it produced. So the man planned to tear down his old barns and built bigger ones to hold it all. He told himself,

> You have plenty of good things laid up for many years. Take life easy; eat, drink and be merry." But then God said to him, "You fool! This very night your life will be demanded from you. Then who will get what you have prepared for yourself? (Luke 12:16–20).

We're never satisfied. We want to have more and more—a bigger house, a newer car, and the latest electronic devices—only to leave it all behind for others to enjoy. I am not one to belittle working hard or having the desire for good things. I do that myself and always have. When I was fourteen, my father told me to get out and get me a job. I asked, "Where am I going to get a job?" He said, "That's your problem. Just go to work." And I have worked ever since. But it is sobering to realize that someday someone else will live in my house and stand behind the pulpits where I preached—and they will sit in your pew.

This truth dawned on me anew a couple of years ago when I served as the executor of a woman's estate. She had a nice house, a new Cadillac, expensive furniture, and huge closets of clothes with five fur coats, ninety pairs of shoes and thousands of dollars in jewelry. It was my responsibility to liquidate all of it for her heirs. The jewelry brought only a fraction of its appraised value. We had an estate sale and sold the furniture for pennies on the dollar. What clothes we couldn't sell we gave to the Salvation Army. All she had accumulated and treasured over a lifetime was gone in a few days. This experience motivated me to clean out my closets and give stuff away. Better to do that now because someday someone else will have to do it for me.

W.T. Waggoner, the Secretary of the Treasury under President Dwight D. Eisenhower, was one of the richest men in Texas. His ranch covered 500,000 acres. He once took a businessman on a tour of his property. Waggoner pointed north and said, "You can ride fifty miles in that direction and still be on my land." Then he pointed to the west, and he said, "You can ride twenty-five miles in that direction and still be on my land."

After Waggoner died, someone asked his business manager, "I wonder how much he left?" The manager answered, "He left it all."

So will we. We all enter and exit life possessing the same thing—nothing. Since things are for time alone and not for eternity, they are never to be of primary value in our lives.

The richest man in America is Bill Gates, the founder of Microsoft. At this writing he is worth 81 billion dollars, and his net worth is growing. Warren Buffet is the second richest man in America. His net worth is 63 billion dollars. Donald Trump is worth a mere 4.5 billion dollars.

That's more than I have! But when I die I will leave as much as Bill Gates, Warren Buffet, and Donald Trump all put together. We'll all leave it all.

The Scriptures teach, "For we brought nothing into the world, and we can take nothing out of it" (1 Timothy 6:7). I relate to the anonymous man who said, "I brought nothing into the world, and I still have most of it."

The Bible warns us that the love of money is the root of every sort of evil and that some people eager for money have "wandered from the faith and pierced themselves with many griefs" (1 Tim. 6:10). It is not money itself but the *love* of money and the *desire* for it that is the root of all evil. You don't have to have it to cause problems, just desire it. If we aren't careful, our obsession with things can cause us to neglect our family, our health, and even God. There is nothing that can replace God quite as easily as the pursuit of possessions.

It's not what you gather but what you scatter that matters in life. In describing a righteous man the Lord says, "He has scattered abroad his gifts to the poor, his righteousness endures forever" (Ps. 112:9; 2 Corinthians 9:9). Then God adds, "Now he who supplies seed to the sower and bread for food will also supply and increase your store of seed and will enlarge the harvest of your righteousness" (2 Cor. 9:10).

Jesus said in his greatest sermon, "Do not store up for yourselves treasures on earth, where moth and rust destroy, and where thieves break in and steal. But store up for yourselves treasures in heaven, where moth and rust do not destroy, and where thieves do not break in and steal" (Matthew 6:19–20).

But how do you do that? Pat Neff, former governor of Texas and later president of Baylor University, once said to the Southern Baptist Convention in Miami, Florida,

> All my life I have heard preachers tell their congregations to lay up treasures in heaven, but none has ever told me exactly how to get my treasures into heaven. I had to figure it out for myself. The only way to get our treasures into heaven is to put them into something that is going to heaven. Cattle, lands, houses, stocks and bonds, oil, coal, and the like are not going to heaven. Only men, women, boys, and girls are going to heaven. Therefore, if I am to lay up treasures in heaven, I must put them to work in the mighty task of redeeming souls that will be fit for heaven!

If a man is growing large in wealth, nothing but constant giving can keep him from growing small in his soul. It's not what you've got but what you do with what you've got that matters (2 Cor. 8:12).

When we talk about giving, some may argue, "But you don't understand the high cost of living." No, it's not the high cost of living; it's the high cost of living the way many of us want to live. It's a matter of priorities and values. If you want to keep balance in your life, learn to give.

Don't Throw away the Ticket

The third and final necessity to stay balanced in life is to believe that no matter how dark the night may be, we are never without hope. When the psalmist wrote these words, he was going through a dark valley. We all do that at times. It is what F. Scott Fitzgerald called "the dark night of the soul."[2] It's easy to stumble and fall in the dark.

In Texas, we say that someone feels "snake bit" when they keep running into bad luck. Have you felt as if you were snake bit? I think the phrase comes from the Old Testament prophet Amos who describes the scene of a man running from a lion who ran into a bear. He ran from the bear and leaned against a wall to rest and a snake bit him. Trouble sometimes comes in droves, and we can't run fast enough to escape it. That's how the psalmist felt.

As I pointed out earlier, his first inclination was to blame someone and lash out at God. That's always a temptation.

When troubles come, we want to fling away faith. But my question is, "Fling it away where?" We are very much in the same position as the disciples who felt they were out of alternatives to following Jesus. When Jesus gave a large group of followers some teachings that were hard to accept, the Bible says that many of them turned and walked with him no more. He then turned to his disciples and asked if they wanted to leave too. Their response was, "Lord, to whom shall we go? You have the words of eternal life" (John 6:68). We, like the disciples, get to the point where we either swim with Jesus, or we sink in despair.

Corrie ten Boom, who endured the atrocities of a Nazi prison camp, often explained, "When a train goes through a tunnel and it gets dark, you don't throw away your ticket and jump off. You sit still and trust the engineer." Elisabeth Elliott, wife of martyred missionary Jim Elliott, also reminds us, "You cannot get to tomorrow morning without going through tonight."[3] If we are going to stay on our feet spiritually and keep from falling into sin, we must anchor our hope in God as well.

In good times of prosperity, we get shortsighted, narrow-minded, and preoccupied with ourselves. Troubles can cause us to step back and assess our lives. That's what happened to the psalmist. He "muses" about his life, and his troubles made him do it. Suddenly he realizes the Lord was never his problem. The Lord was his hope (Ps. 39:7). In the same way, we need to step back occasionally to evaluate what's going on, and trouble helps us to do that. I have heard it said that power brings us the praise of man, but weakness brings us to God. That's what we need.

No matter how dark the night might be there is always hope. The Scriptures point us to our ultimate hope, the eternal God. Moses said, "The eternal God is your refuge, and underneath are the everlasting arms" (Deuteronomy 33:27). The Puritans used to say, "Lay your life at the Lord's feet, and he will take you in his arms." You can do that very thing today. Paul says we are to "rest on the hope of eternal life, which God, who does not lie, promised before the beginning of time" (Titus 1:2). If our lives are rooted in God through faith in Jesus Christ, they are never in vain. Because he lives, we shall live also. Our brief days shall soon pass, and our possessions will be left behind. Yet Jesus said the one "who does the will of God lives forever" (1 John 2:17). That is our eternal hope—a hope that shines brightly no matter how dark the night.

NOTES

1. Originally printed in the *Florida Times-Union*, March 31, 2015.
2. F. Scott Fitzgerald, Edmund Wilson, ed., *The Crack-Up* (New York, NY: New Directions, 2009), 75.
3. http://www.ligonier.org/learn/articles/theres-no-coming-life-without-pain-interview-elisabeth-elliot/. Accessed 1/5/16.

The more the leaves around us fall,
the more we wonder,
"Is this all there is to life?
Am I living my life to the full?"
The good news of Christ is that
even if we haven't done so yet,
we can make the most
of what's left.

2

Make the Most of What's Left

Philippians 3:13–14

Sometimes people aren't who they seem to be. J. Edgar Hoover, considered America's foremost law enforcement official, was director of the Federal Bureau of Investigation for forty-eight years. It's now been revealed that Hoover apparently had ties with the Mafia, the gambling industry, and the homosexual community. Though Hoover denied the existence of syndicated crime in America, many historians have argued that he received favors such as food and lodging from mob figures and that he was an avid gambler. If he lost at the casinos, they gave him his money back. If he won, he kept his winnings.

He kept extensive surveillance records on eight presidents and many other politicians with whom he served, and they continued to reappointment him for fear of blackmail. I've heard it said of his life that Hoover performed his greatest public service when he died.

Sometimes people's lives are not what they seem to be. Once one of the most respected men in America, Hoover kept secrets that prevented him from being the man we thought he was. We all have things in our lives that can keep us from making the most of our time. The good news of the gospel is that regardless of our past, we don't have to stay the way we are. We can't go back and relive the past, but we can start where we are and, with God's help, make the most of what's left . . . even if we've had a wonderfully blessed life thus far.

The Apostle Paul wrote of his own life, " . . . Forgetting what is behind and straining toward what is ahead, I press on toward the goal to win the prize for which God has called me heavenward in Christ Jesus" (Philippians 3:13–14). Paul would likely describe his life as difficult but glorious. However, he was neither focused on, nor satisfied with the past. He was determined to keep progressing, making the most of what was left, and advancing until the last leaf had fallen. We find that we can follow that same desire to seize life's opportunities when we understand three principles:

- We need something to live for.
- We need a self to live with.
- We need a Savior to lean on.

In Jesus' Name, Amen! 

First, we need something to live for—something or someone bigger and beyond ourselves. Knowing our purpose in life and our reason for living gives us staying power and the ability to go on, even in the face of adversity.

In *The Greatest Generation*, Tom Brokaw tells of how men in World War II repeatedly endured prison, abuse, and the carnage of war because of a girl they were going home to marry, their parents, or some tangible hope that gave them a reason to live. Likewise, Swiss psychiatrist Viktor Frankl wrote in *Man's Search for Meaning* about how people endured the most inhumane, degrading, and incredible suffering in Nazi concentration camps when they had some compelling reason to live—their children, a book they wanted to write, or a specific talent they could use. Frankl was also fond of quoting Friedrich Nietzsche, who observed, "He who has a why to live can bear with almost any how."

What is the "why" of your life? What keeps you going? What is your reason for living? There is just one cause worthy of your highest and best. That's the cause of Jesus Christ, the pearl of great price and the treasure found in a field (Matthew 13:44–46). It's the one thing that's worth everything. Jesus put it this way, "For whoever wants to save his life will lose it, but whoever loses his life for me and for the gospel will save it" (Mark 8:35).

There is a God-shaped vacuum—a hole in the soul—that nothing smaller than God can fill. Until we have him in our lives, we start at no beginning and we work to no end.

Without any other worthy purpose or commitment in life, people keep trying to fill their inner emptiness with substitutes like material possessions—houses, cars, clothes, jewelry, land, and gadgets of all kinds. Jesus warned us about the deceitfulness of riches (Mark 4:19). Wealth presents the illusion that we will be happy if we just have enough of it. But things cannot fill the emptiness in us. So people end up with everything to live with, and nothing to live for.

Others try to substitute God with pleasure. They live for the weekend, quitting time, and a chance to go to the bar or the ball game. The Scriptures say those who live for pleasure are actually dead while they live (1 Timothy 5:6). The next time you're sitting in a restaurant or in a stadium seat, look around carefully; you may be sitting next to a dead person. They're physically alive but dead on the inside. They're spiritually dead and they don't know it.

Still others live for their own self-advancement, striving for prominence and position. Historian Ken Burns produced a documentary, *The Roosevelts: An Intimate History*, and said of President Theodore Roosevelt, "He wanted to be the bride at every wedding, the corpse at every funeral, and the baby at every christening." Likewise, Burns described Theodore's cousin Franklin Delano as having "lived all his life being thought of as number one." There are people who spend their lives trying to climb the ladder of success—either the corporate ladder or the social ladder—only to realize when they get to the top that it is leaning against the wrong wall.

Jesus warned against that kind of self-promotion and worldly ambition, saying that those who exalt themselves will be brought low (Matt. 23:12). Take a backseat and let others promote you. That's the better way to get to the head table.

None of these things fully satisfies, and they leave many people disillusioned. Herodotus claimed that the bitterest sorrow a man can know is to aspire to do much and to achieve nothing. Carlyle Marney, a Baptist preacher and professor, disagreed, saying, "The bitterest sorrow is to aspire to do much and to do it and then to discover it was not worth doing." Jesus calls us to live for his sake and the gospel (Mark 8:35). Put your faith in Jesus so he can enable you to make the most of what's left of your life.

Joe Foss is just one of many who found the secret to a meaningful life this way. He was the quintessential World War II hero. When the Japanese bombed Pearl Harbor, he was quick to join the Marines. Already an experienced pilot, he was soon shipped to Guadalcanal as an executive officer of Marine F–4 Wildcat fighter planes. Within a week, he had shot down his first Japanese Zero. Within a month, he had shot down twenty-three.

When he returned from one mission, his ground crew counted more than 200 bullet holes in his plane. Within a year, he had shot down twenty-six enemy planes equaling Eddie Rickenbacker's record of World War I. For his heroics he was awarded the Congressional Medal of Honor.

Returning home to his native South Dakota, he became involved in politics and was elected governor of South Dakota. A troubled marriage cost him a second term, but he went on to become the first commissioner of the fledging American Football League.

Then he married DiDi, who helped lead him to the life-changing experience of becoming an enthusiastic born again Christian. He said in an interview with Brokaw, "For an old whiskey-drinking, cigar-smoking, master of profanity who had been an absentee father and husband for much of his first marriage, this was a complete makeover."[1]

He told Brokaw that his embrace of the Lord was "the greatest decision I ever made and I made it for eternity." Thereafter in every speech he made, he mentioned the Lord. And he always ended his speeches with, "In Jesus' name, Amen."

Some of his friends took him aside and said, "Joe maybe you ought to leave Jesus out."

Joe responded, "'No, sir!' I tell 'em."

Joe found his life worth living when he found Jesus, and so can you.

The secret to finding purpose in life is committing that whatever you do, you'll do it all for the glory of God (1 Corinthians 10:31). Just do it in Jesus' name, Amen!

I Like You and I Like Me 

We need something to live for, but we also need a self to live with. The second principle of making the most of what's left of our lives is learning to like ourselves, respect ourselves, and be at peace with who we are. One time as I was visiting my grandson when he was just a little boy, I leaned over and whispered in his ear, "I sure do like you." He replied, "Me, too. I like you and I like me." Now that's a good self-image. But a lot of people don't like themselves and that is tragic.

It's hard to make the most of what's left if we find it difficult to like ourselves. Life has ways of chipping away at our self-image. For example, sometimes other people do it to us. A book about Winston Churchill, *The Last Lion*, tells of the great suffering the people of Europe endured during the 1930s. Churchill recalls how the Nazis rounded up people walking the streets of Prater, Czechoslovakia, one Sunday and separated the Jews from the rest of the crowd. They made the Jewish gentlemen take off all their clothes and walk on all fours on the grass. Then they forced the Jewish ladies to climb ladders into some trees and chirp like birds. The number of suicides resulting from psychological torture by the Nazis was appalling. Churchill, commenting on their cruelty, wrote, "You may take a man's life, but to destroy all his dignity is bestial."[2]

Humiliation and the degrading of human personality and personal dignity can happen in more subtle ways. If you live with constant criticism; if people make fun of how you look or where you live; if they call you names—that will do it. Abuse, whether physical, sexual, or verbal, can eventually beat down even the strongest person. The injustice may come from a parent, a husband or wife, or a classmate. People can embarrass us, humiliate us, and degrade us until we feel we are worthless nobodies.

I once read about a woman who escaped an eight-year abusive relationship with a man. She said, "I met a man that was what I like to call a 'counterfeit.' He looked great, made me feel good . . . but he had a darker side, and over time I learned to hide the pain, the bruises, the abuse, the violence, and in that process I shut down. I closed my heart, my mind, my soul, everything and to everyone. For many years, I felt unworthy—unworthy of love, unworthy of life, unworthy of being a human being . . . Even though it was not (physically) abusive, just verbal, it was very prevalent in my life."[3]

Sometimes we do it to ourselves. We fail (or feel that we have failed) as a parent, as a mate, or in our profession. Or maybe you're addicted to alcohol, drugs, pornography, or an uncontrolled temper. (I do not mean an "uncontrollable" temper because all temper can be controlled unless a person is mentally ill.) You can be involved in these activities until you hate yourself. You may have promised yourself a thousand times that you were going to quit, but like a dog who returns to his vomit, you repeatedly go back to the very thing that makes you sick (Proverbs 26:11; 2 Peter 2:22).

Alternately, you may be living a lie. You are not who people think you are—your parents, your children, your mate, your neighbors, your fellow workers, or your church friends. They think you are an honest, faithful, and upright person, but you know better. And the guilt and fear that other people know the truth about you keep weighing you down. The result is self-hatred.

Jesus gives us the answer to self-hatred and a poor self-image in the Lord's Prayer. "Forgive us our debts as we also have forgiven our debtors" (Matt. 6:12). First, we must ask

God to forgive us for our sins. Then we must forgive others who have wronged us. To hold on to hate and bitterness is like holding a lighted match. Hold it long enough and you are the one who will be burned.

The good news of the gospel is that you can be forgiven. You can be clean again, and you can start afresh. The Scriptures say, "If we confess our sins, he is faithful and just and will forgive us our sins, and purify us from all unrighteousness" (1 John 1:9).

John Newton, who wrote the wonderful hymn *Amazing Grace*, was once the captain of a slave ship. When his ship was caught in a terrible storm and he thought he was going to die, he promised God that he would change if God saved him. The Lord did rescue him that day, and Newton eventually became a very effective minister for Christ and built a great church in Olney, England. Having lost his eyesight late in life, he dictated in his memoirs, "I am an old man and I have forgotten many things. I do remember I was a great sinner and I have a great savior."[4] God's forgiving grace enables us to put the past behind us and live free. That's why John Newton could write such a great hymn about grace.

The other half of what Jesus taught us in the Lord's Prayer is that we must then forgive others who have hurt us. No matter what they have done, we can and must forgive them. Many people do not understand forgiveness. It is not the same as forgetting. If others wrong you, and you choose to forgive them, it means that you suffer the loss and they go free. You do not try to get even with them or make them pay for what they have done. Real forgiveness not only frees them, but also frees you from anger and resentment.

You can be reconciled to God and to others. You can be forgiven. You can start over and try again because God is the God of a second chance. If you are right with God and with others, you can then be right with yourself. However, you will not find life worthwhile until you like yourself. You will not be at peace with yourself until you are at peace with God and with others.

Lean On Me

The third and final key to seizing the opportunities we have left in life is to realize we need a Savior to lean on. Buckner Fanning, longtime pastor of Trinity Baptist Church in San Antonio, Texas, told a story in *God Drives a Pickup Truck* about his church building a rehabilitation house for women suffering from chronic alcohol and substance abuse. The home began small, but through the years it expanded to minister to 200 women who had experienced physical, spiritual, and emotional healing.

One day "Jane," the director of the home, brought a new resident to Buckner's office for a visit. "Mary" had seen him on television and expressed a desire to talk with him personally.

After they had visited together briefly, he writes, "I began to tell Mary that she could lean on God for help. I never finished the sentence. When she heard the phrase 'if you will just lean on God'—she exploded!

"Mary's eyes flashed with anger as she harshly said, 'Don't tell me to lean on God. I'm not about to lean on God. Every time I've gone near a church or a bunch of Christians they put me down. They make me feel worthless and rejected. I don't want to have anything to do with God or church people. In fact I don't even believe in God at all.'

"I was stunned into silence. A verbal detonation had rocked me back on my heels. I was speechless. I just sat there.

"Jane, seated beside Mary on the couch, gently placed her hand on the hand of the angry young woman. Softly she said, 'It's alright, if you don't believe in God, that's alright. I understand. You don't have to lean on God. Why don't you just lean on me and I'll lean on God.'"

According to Buckner, in time God's love began to grow in Mary's life, and one Sunday morning during the invitation she came down the aisle with tears streaming down her face and said, "I love him and I trust him."

Buckner writes, "Jane came forward to sit beside Mary, as she had sat beside her on the couch in my office months before. Once again, Jane reached out and held Mary's hand. Jane had become an angel to lean on."[5]

But more than that, they were both now leaning on Jesus.

We all need someone else to lean on. Sometimes it's a Christian friend, but most of all we need to lean on Jesus like John reclining on Christ's breast at the Last Supper (John 13:25). Jesus says to lean on him and he will get us through whatever life hurls at us. He'll get us through our dark nights of the soul, our Gethsemane of loneliness and abandonment, and our Calvary of suffering and death.

Then with something to live for, a self to live with, and a Savior to lean on, we can make the most of what's left of life.

NOTES

1. Tom Brokaw, *The Greatest Generation* (New York, NY: Random House Trade Paperbacks, 2001), 115–124.
2. William Manchester, *The Last Lion: Winston Spencer Churchill: Defender of the Realm, 1940–1945* (New York, NY: Bantam Books, 2013), 306.
3. *Tyler Morning Telegraph,* October, 29, 2014.
4. A. Maxwell, *Memoirs of the Rev. John Newton* (London, England, 1813).
5. Buckner Fanning, *God Drives a Pickup Truck* (Indianapolis, IN: LifeWorks Publishing, 1999), 91–94.

Ralph Waldo Emerson described Jesus as one "whose name is not so much written as ploughed into the history of this world." The more we honor him, the better our lives will be.

3

Honor Jesus

William Wilberforce left an enduring example of what it means to honor Jesus. The great British reformer served in Parliament from 1784–1812 and was also a politician, philanthropist, and theologian. After serving as a member of Parliament, he became a Christian under the influence of John Newton. Wilberforce immediately wanted to go into the ministry. However, Newton persuaded him that he could do more for the cause of the Lord by remaining in politics rather than in the ministry. So Wilberforce gave himself to making England a better country.

He wrote in his diary, "God has set before me two great objectives: the suppression of the slave trade in the British Empire and the reformation of [morals]."[1] Every year for twenty years he stood in Parliament and made an impassioned plea that slavery be abolished, and every year for twenty years they voted him down. Three days before he died, the British Empire abolished slavery.

In addition to this landmark achievement, his philanthropic work was also legendary. Kevin Belmonte wrote in *A Journey Through the Life of William Wilberforce* that good causes "stuck to him like pins to a magnet." For example, he helped to establish soup kitchens; libraries; and schools for the poor, deaf, and blind. He also supported vaccinations for smallpox, prison reform, and efforts to improve working conditions. He helped to establish hospitals, a society for the prevention of cruelty to animals, and worked tirelessly to distribute Bibles around the world.

When he died, friends in Parliament requested that he be buried in Westminster Abbey. As the Duke of Wellington walked amid the funeral procession, some in the crowd recognized him and started to cheer him. Before they could applaud, the Duke raised his finger to his lips in a silent but proud admonition. It was, said a witness, as though the great man were saying: "You're not here to honor me but him whom I have come to honor." Likewise, if we want to make the most of our lives, we must determine to honor Jesus throughout our days and no one else.

On the eighth day after his birth, Jesus was circumcised and named as the angel had instructed. A Jewish woman was considered unclean for forty days after childbirth. However, the Law required a sacrifice at the temple—generally a lamb and a turtledove or pigeon. If the person was especially poor, two pigeons were acceptable. That's all Mary and Joseph offered, given their humble circumstances.

The aged priest serving in the temple that day was named Simeon. The Lord had previously revealed to Simeon that he would not die until he had seen the Savior, the Messiah who would deliver Israel and restore the kingdom of David. Every day, he had looked forward to God's redemption and the literal reestablishment of that kingdom. So when Mary and Joseph placed baby Jesus in his arms, he told God he was ready to die now that his "eyes have seen your salvation" (Luke 2:30). Then he praised Jesus in a simple but straightforward way (Luke 2:31–35). In this brief tribute, he paid honor to Jesus by affirming three characteristics of his nature:

- He is the glory of Israel.
- He is the light of the Gentiles.
- He is the Savior of the world.

The Glory of Israel

First, Simeon said that Jesus is the glory of Israel. What does that mean? Israel is an enigma in history, so why should it occupy such a prominent place in world affairs? It is a small Middle Eastern country only 120 miles long at its longest point, sixty miles at its widest point, and barely thirty-five miles wide at its narrowest point. By comparison with the United States, it is about the size of New Jersey and nineteen times smaller than California. Israel is also surrounded by twenty-two hostile Arab-Islamic countries, all awash with oil and all wanting to destroy the Jewish nation. It is the most fought over piece of soil on earth.

What then is the "glory of Israel"? It is certainly not its size or its wealth. It is not because it is the only democracy in the region (or even the only Jewish state). It is the fact that it was, and is, the birthplace of the Messiah.

We must go back in history 4,000 years to the time of Abraham to understand this truth. The Scriptures explain that God called Abraham from Ur of the Chaldeans and promised to make him a great nation, give him a great name, and make him a great blessing so that through him all the nations on the earth would be blessed (Genesis 12:1–2).

Later, the Lord told Abraham, "All the land that you see I will give to you and your offspring forever" (Gen. 13:15). But this promise to make him a great nation could not be fulfilled unless Abraham had a son, and his wife, Sarah, was barren. So Abraham took matters into his own hands and had an illegitimate child with his servant girl, Hagar, and named him Ishmael. Isaac, through whom the blessing would come, would be born later, but Ishmael would become the father of the Arabs. Scripture predicted at Ishmael's birth, "He will be a wild donkey of a man; his hand will be against everyone and everyone's hand against him; and he will live in hostility toward all his brothers" (Gen. 16:12).

From the beginning, Ishmael was a problem to the children of Israel. His descendants, the Arabs, have been antagonistic to the Jews throughout both biblical (Nehemiah 2:19; 6:1–2) and secular history. Today they are troubling the whole world. Their hands seem to be against everyone. However, this original prophecy was not fully realized until 570–632 AD when Islam was established under Mohammed.

God's promise to Abraham lingered unfulfilled for nearly 2,000 years. "But when the time had fully come, God sent his Son, born of a woman, born under law, to redeem those under law, that we might receive the full rights of sons" (Galatians 4:4–5). The Jews were always a stubborn and rebellious people and hard to govern. Rome ruled Israel when Jesus was born, and they eventually crucified him. In the year 70 AD, the Roman Emperor Titus destroyed the city of Jerusalem, burned the temple, and killed more than a million Jews. The only part of the temple that still exists today is the Western Wall (often called the Wailing Wall). The Jews rebelled again in 135 AD, and this time a half a million of them were killed. The rest were scattered to the four winds. Virtually all the Jews had left Israel by the year 200 AD, and the land was renamed Palestine.

They continued being driven from their homeland until the 20th century when the United Nations established the state of Israel. A number of countries had ruled Israel through the years, but it was under the control of Turkey during World War II. Turkey, an ally of Germany, surrendered Israel to the control of England when the Germans lost the war. The English allowed it to be reestablished as a Jewish state by the United Nations in 1948.

Despite this turbulent history, it's amazing that the Jews maintained their national identity and their allegiance to the land for almost 1,900 years. Though they had no country of their own, they still kept hope alive that they would return someday. In his book *The Gift of Rest*, Senator Joe Lieberman suggests that the Jews' faithful observance of the Sabbath Day was one of the things that helped maintain their national identity. Orthodox Jews observe the Sabbath from sundown on Friday until sundown on Saturday. Lieberman also explains that when they prepare the Sabbath meal, they prepare spiritually for the arrival of the most eminent of guests—the King of Kings. On the Sabbath, he says, Jews feel they are welcoming God into their homes with gratitude and love. Then he quotes Rabbi Ahad Ha'am: "More than the Jews have kept the Sabbath, the Sabbath has kept the Jews."

Moreover, they close the Passover meal with the phrase, "Next year in Jerusalem." Jerusalem is more than just a geographical place; it is a symbol of the coming Messiah. With these continuous practices in place for generations, how could they not have maintained their identity or their loyalty to Israel? The Lord entrusted them as the people of God to give birth to the Messiah and to the gospel for the benefit of the whole world. If the Lord had not entrusted them with this divine mission, they would likely be just another Bedouin tribe of the Near East.

We are better able to give Jesus the honor he is due when we understand history and see him as he really is—the glory of Israel.

A Light in the Dark 

Second, Simeon described Jesus as the light of the Gentiles (non-Jews). There are two kinds of light. There is physical light by which we see the world. God said, "Let there be light" on the first day of Creation. There is also spiritual light by which we understand truth, and this light is in the heart and mind of each person. God placed it there (Romans 2:15).

As if that was not enough, God also gave us the light of his word. "Your word is a lamp to my feet and a light for my path" (Psalm 119:105). The Lord made Israel a spiritual light for all Gentiles (Isaiah 42:6). He did not pour out his favor and blessings on Israel because he liked them more than any other people. He simply intended for them to serve as his missionaries and carry the gospel to all nations.

This, however, became the source of their failure. Jesus pointed out this truth one day in his hometown of Nazareth. As was his custom, he went to synagogue on the Sabbath. They recognized Jesus as a rabbi and invited him to read the Scriptures and deliver a message. He took his text from Isaiah where God spoke of the Messiah and read aloud,

> The Spirit of the Sovereign LORD is on me, because the LORD has anointed me to preach good news to the poor. He has sent me to bind up the brokenhearted, to proclaim freedom for the captives and release from darkness for the prisoners, to proclaim the year of the LORD's favor and

> the day of vengeance of our God, to comfort all who mourn . . . (Isa. 61:1–2).

Afterwards, he told the congregation that he had fulfilled what they just heard.

The people could not believe their ears. They had seen Jesus growing up in their village—how could he be the Messiah in their midst? So they immediately rejected him. In response, Jesus highlighted two experiences from the Old Testament to demonstrate how the Jews were not helping Jewish widows or Gentile lepers as they should. He shared how the prophet Elijah blessed the Gentile widow from Zarephath in a time of drought (1 Kings 17:8–16). By God's miraculous power, her bowl of meal never dried up; her vial of oil never diminished. Then he told about an experience from the life of Elisha where he healed a leprous Gentile named Naaman, the captain of the Syrian army (2 Kings 5:1–14).

However, it's what he said about God "doing for the Gentiles what he didn't do for the Jews" that made the people of Nazareth so angry that they wanted to lynch him. They believed that *they* were God's people, and they despised others. In fact, they felt that God had created the Gentiles to be fuel for the fires of hell. Instead of being a light to others, the Jews had slowly become proud, exclusive, and prejudiced.

The gospel is for everyone, especially the excluded and oppressed elements of society. Yet this kind of gospel message inflames prideful people. That's one reason why Jesus was crucified.

Jesus, the glory of Israel and the Jews, is also the light of the Gentiles. We must give him the honor due his name.

It Cost Him His Life 

The third reason why we honor Jesus is that he is also the Savior of the world. I once heard that when legendary Methodist pastor Halford Luccock asked his two granddaughters what they wanted for Christmas, they responded, "Give us a world." Puzzled by such a request, he consulted their mother who explained that the girls wanted a globe. However, when the girls opened his gift that held the globe, he could sense they were a bit disappointed. Finally, one of them explained, "We were hoping it would be a lighted world."

"Oh, I can fix that," he assured them. He returned the globe to the store to trade it for one with lights inside.

When he presented the new globe to the girls, they were thrilled. In recalling what he learned from this experience, he later commented to a friend, "I learned that a lighted world costs a lot more." If we want to light the world for Jesus, we must realize that it will cost us more. Yet it cost Jesus much more as well.

In fact, when Simeon blessed Mary and Joseph at the end of their visit, he predicted that suffering was ahead. He told Mary,

> This child is destined to cause the falling and rising of many in Israel, and to be a sign that will

> be spoken against, so that the thoughts of many hearts will be revealed. And a sword will pierce your own soul too (Luke 2:34–35).

In other words, those who believed in him would be lifted from their sin, while those who rejected him would fall into despair and darkness. Jesus would bring judgment as well as salvation to the world.

Seneca, the Greek philosopher, said, "What men need above all is a hand to reach down and lift them up." That's what we have in Jesus Christ. But this gift cost him his life, just as the prophet Isaiah described.

> He was despised and rejected by men, a man of sorrows, and familiar with suffering. Like one from whom men hide their faces he was despised, and we esteemed him not. Surely he took up our infirmities and carried our sorrows, yet we considered him stricken by God, smitten by him, and afflicted. But he was pierced for our transgressions, he was crushed for our iniquities; the punishment that brought us peace was upon him, and by his wounds we are healed. We all, like sheep, have gone astray, each of us has turned to his own way; and the LORD has laid on him the iniquity of us all (Isa. 53:3–6).

Today we often explain the cost in a very familiar verse: "For God so loved the world that he gave his one and only Son, that whoever believes in him shall not perish but have eternal life" (John 3:16). Jesus is worthy of our greatest honor for he is the glory of Israel; he is the light of the Gentiles; and he is the Savior of the world. This is reason enough for us to trust him and follow him as Lord and Master.

NOTES

1. John Pollock, *Wilberforce* (London, England: Constable, 1977).

*The older we grow by his grace,
the more we need to understand
and rejoice in his grace.*

4

Grow Old Gracefully

Isaiah 46:4

In what may be one of the greatest novels of all time, *The Count of Monte Cristo* by Alexandre Dumas, we find a story of hope, justice, mercy, and forgiveness. Edmond Dantés is a young and successful merchant who returns to Marseille to marry his fiancé. Soon, however, another suitor and two of his friends falsely accuse him. He lands in prison for thirteen years where he seethes in anger, plotting his revenge.

He even carves on the wall of his cell, "God will give me justice."

As the story unfolds, a priest befriends him in prison and tells Dantés one day, "God will help you."

Hardened by his circumstances, Dantés retorts, "But I don't believe in God."

The priest then wisely responds, "Yes, but he believes in you."

That's the message of the Bible—God believes in us. In his autobiography, a British actor named Forbes-Robertson tells a similar story about an ardent atheist named Crow in his London club who constantly voiced his disbelief in Christ until one of the members jotted a few lines for him:

> We've heard in language highly spiced,
> That Crow does not believe in Christ,
> But what we're more concerned to know,
> Is whether Christ believes in Crow.[1]

As we go through life, we often feel abandoned, forsaken, and alone. Nevertheless, we are never alone because God still believes in us. Let the changes that take place drive you to the One who never changes. The Bible says, "Even to your old age and gray hairs I am he, I am he who will sustain you. I have made you and I will carry you; I will sustain you and I will rescue you" (Isaiah 46:4). How much does God believe in you? Isaiah shares three great responses to that question in this passage:

- He believes in you enough to have created you.

- He believes in you enough to sustain you.
- He believes in you enough to save you.

You Are Nearest and Dearest to God

The first truth assures you that God believed in you enough to create you in the first place. A little girl once asked her mother, "How did the human race appear?" The mother answered, "God made Adam and Eve, and they had children, and so was all humankind made."

Two days later the little girl asked her father the same question. The father answered, "Many years ago there were monkeys from which the human race evolved."

The confused girl returned to her mother and said, "Mom, how is it possible that you told me the human race was created by God and Dad said we developed from monkeys?"

The mother answered, "Well, dear, it's very simple. I told you about my side of the family, and your father told you about his."

I don't know where your side of the family came from, but we all came from God! Genesis opens the account of Creation with the words, "In the *beginning* . . ."—whenever that was. The Bible does not date Creation. I will let the geologist tell me *when* it all happened, if he will let me tell him *who* made it happen.

Genesis goes on to say, "In the beginning *God* . . ." The Hebrew word for "God" is Elohim. The root meaning of the word is "power." God is the One to whom all power belongs.

"In the beginning God *created the heavens and the earth* . . ." The Hebrew word for "created" is "bara," which means to create from nothing. We can take a load of wood and make a house. We can take a load of steel and make a car. But only God can take nothing and make everything. That's the way all of creation came into being.

There is, of course, another theory that claims that the universe made itself. In other words, matter is eternal. In the eons of time, there was an explosion in space called the Big Bang. Life then emerged by spontaneous generation and evolved from the simple to the complex.

The choice is between divine revelation or human speculation. Creation happened only once. It can't be repeated, and no one was there to see it except God. So we either take his word for it, or we guess at it. The theory of evolution is a guess.

If there was a big bang in space, God was the big banger. In Genesis, he does not attempt to give us a detailed, scientific account of Creation. It is a mere outline. He does not make any claims beyond this: "By faith we understand that the universe was formed by God's command" (Hebrews 11:3). The message of Genesis is simple: God is the agent of Creation. He created all things separate and distinct, starting with the simple and moving to the complex before finally making us in his own image. We are, therefore, the nearest and dearest to God.

I don't know exactly what the Bible means by God making us in his image, but I do know that humans are unique in many ways. Humans are the only animals that clothe themselves and the only ones that bury their dead. They are the only animals that commit suicide and the only ones capable of being bored with their existence. The only animals that war and the only ones with the power of imagination to advance civilization. Humans are the only animals that both laugh and cry because they are the only ones that know the difference between the way things are and how things ought to be. And humans are the only animals that worship.

God really does believe in us. He didn't have to create us. The world got along just fine before we arrived, and it will do fine after we are gone. However, he *wanted* us. If he took the time to create us, he will also keep us going—as we learn in the next point.

As a Father Carries His Son 

The second truth we learn from the passage in Isaiah is that God believes in us enough to sustain us. When I was at a retreat with Park Cities Baptist Church, a lady told me the story of Dottie Fanoni, a longtime foreign missionary who knew God as her sustainer. As Dottie grew old, the doctor said that she must go to a nursing home. But her financial advisor countered that she did not have enough money to do that.

She said to him matter-of-factly, "Haven't you learned by now that God is going to take care of me?" Within a few weeks, she died at age eighty-seven. The Lord took care of her; she didn't have to worry about paying for a nursing home. Her Bible was well-read and held together with duct tape. Although she may not have had much financially, she had two prayer lists of six or seven pages each and a God who cared for her.

When I was interim pastor of First Baptist Church in Tyler, Texas, we broadcast our services on television. An elderly lady from Athens, Texas, watched our services regularly and often wrote me notes of encouragement. I always responded with a personal note to her. She wrote on one occasion that she hoped to meet me some day, so one day I left an hour early to visit her on my way south to Waco. She lived in an old, rundown mobile home on a country road near the edge of town. When I knocked on the front door and there was no answer, I went to the back door. Still no answer. I circled back to the front, and as I was writing a note to leave her, she came to the door in a wheelchair. As we visited, without complaint or bitterness, she explained that her only daughter lived in a distant state and she was all alone. As we talked about life and the Lord, she assured me, "Pastor, the Lord sustains me." Can you say the same in your life's circumstances?

The Lord says to us through Moses that he carries us "as a father carries his son" (Deuteronomy 1:31). He carries us even when we can no longer carry ourselves. That's how much he believes in us.

From Dust to Dust 

If you're still not convinced that the Lord believes in you, remember that he cared enough to save you. This is the final truth we learn in Isaiah. The word "rescue" means "to redeem, to preserve, to save." In Isaiah, the word is used to speak of our future hope.

The only thing that comes to us without effort is old age. In fact, Canadian humorist Richard J. Needham is said to have identified seven ages of man: spills, drills, thrills, bills, ills, pills, and wills. The Apostle Paul, describing the trials of a missionary's life, tells us why he never gave up. "Therefore we do not lose heart. Though outwardly we are wasting away, yet inwardly we are being renewed day by day" (2 Corinthians 4:16).

There is an outer you—your body, your reputation, your persona; and there is an inner you—your character, your spirit, and your soul. The outer you is what everybody sees; the inner you is invisible. The outer you is temporary; the inner you is eternal. Like it or not, the outer you is perishing day-by-day.

Consider that from age twenty-five our bones begin to lose calcium and get more brittle. Our skin begins to lose its elasticity and shrivel. Age spots begin to multiply, and gray strands of hair begin to appear. (Fortunately, you have over one hundred billion of them.) After age thirty, we lose over 1,000 brain cells every day. Our weight starts shifting from the poles of our body toward our equator. And there's nothing we can do about it. We can fight it, but we can't win. We can spend money on it and invest time in it. You can exercise it, starve it, Botox it, stretch it, tuck it, lift it, and dress it up, but you came from dust, and unto dust you will return. Eventually the outer you simply wears out.

But the good news is that if our earthly "house" dissolves, we have a building of God not made with human hands that is eternal in heaven (2 Cor. 5:1–4). To put it another way, our body is like a tent that can wear out, sag, and be blown away. When that happens, we receive a new everlasting home in heaven.

One day when I was getting dressed, I looked in the mirror and thought to myself, "Everything I have was made by someone else, somewhere else." The pants I was wearing were made in Mexico. The tie was made in Italy. The shirt, Bangladesh. The belt, China. And the shoes I wore were made in Brazil. I was the only thing made in the USA. Yet one day I will have a new body not made with human hands but by God's workmanship.

The Scriptures say that Abraham by faith looked for a city with foundations whose architect and contractor was God (Heb. 11:10). Abraham lived in a tent with no foundation. Stakes held it in the ground that could easily be taken up, moved, and put down again. By contrast, God's eternal home for us is the same city described in the Book of Revelation. John writes, "I saw the Holy City, the new Jerusalem, coming down out of heaven from God, prepared as a bride beautifully dressed for her husband" (Revelation 21:2). And what a wonderful city it will be.

Some people spend their lives planning their dream home, only to trade it for a nursing home. To all of us Jesus said, "I go to prepare a place for you" (John 14:2). And it is a permanent home.

For which home are you preparing?

Dr. Harry Schwensberg and his wife, Dorothy, were pioneers of our Southern Baptist mission work in Columbia, South America, for thirty years. After they completed their assignment there, they served in Spain another fifteen years. When they retired, they came to live in Tyler, Texas, in the Green Acres Missionary Home. Harry continued to be active in missionary work, especially in Mexico, because he spoke Spanish so well. On returning from such a trip, one of our men asked him if he was afraid to die. He replied, "No, but I am afraid of living too long." And he did. As he grew old, he moved into his daughter's house where he was bedridden for a number of years. He said to her one day, "I'm ready to go home."

She replied, "Papa, you are home."

He then pointed up to heaven and repeated, "I am ready to go *home*."

She assured him again, "But Papa, your mansion is not ready yet."

At this, Harry said, "I'll take it like it is."

I can assure you that your heavenly home is ready. Jesus has gone to prepare it, and we have his word for it. He believes in you enough to have created you, sustain you, and save you if you will trust in him. I hope you believe in God. But even if you don't, he believes in you.

NOTES

1. Johnston Forbes-Robertson, *A Player Under Three Reigns* (1925) referenced in *Riverside Sermons*, Harry Emmerson Fosdick, (New York, NY: Harper and Brothers, 1958), 305.

Whoever first said, "Old age is not for sissies" knew what he was talking about. Suffering has no expiration date on it. The question, "Why do bad things happen to good people?" never goes away. Job deals with this issue in his own life and helps us to deal with it in ours.

5

Hang on During Hard Times

Job 13:15

Why do bad things happen to good people? It's a question as old as recorded history. It is also the central concern in the book of Job, the oldest book in the Bible and, some believe, the oldest book in existence.

Job was a real person who lived before or during the period of the Patriarchs. He was not just a good man—he was one of the best men who ever lived. He revered God and avoided every kind of evil. There was hardly a cloud in Job's sky. He had a godly character, a sterling reputation, a large and loving family, and fabulous wealth with herds of camels, sheep, and donkeys.

Satan, who is also a real person and the adversary of God's people, appears in the story without introduction or explanation. He accused Job of serving God only because God had been so good to him. He even suggested that Job's faith would falter if God would let him bring trouble into Job's life. Satan is powerful but not all-powerful. He can do only what God permits him to do. God permits him to test our faith, just as he tested the faith of Jesus.

At this point, storm clouds gathered over Job's life. First, he lost all his livestock to thieves and tragedy. Then a tornado struck a house, killing his ten children inside. When word came to Job about these catastrophes, he fell on his knees to worship God. He affirmed his confidence in the Lord saying, "Naked I came from my mother's womb, and naked I will depart. The Lord gave and the Lord has taken away; may the name of the Lord be praised" (Job 1:21). Job neither sinned against God nor blamed him for his troubles.

Satan, however, was not easily discouraged. He stayed on the attack with Job as he does with us. Next he wanted to afflict his health, thinking that would do the trick. Once again God gave him permission to test the faith of his servant. He would allow Satan's request, with the exception that he could not take Job's life.

Soon painful boils covered Job's body. His wife, whose faith was not as strong as her husband's, took note of his miserable condition and suggested that he curse God and die. But Job reproved her as a foolish woman, asking if it was right to "accept good from God, and not trouble" (Job 2:10).

Once again Job did not sin against God by accusing or cursing him. Clearly, God's confidence in this good man's faith had been vindicated. But by then Job's reputation was in question. Friends wondered what bad thing he had done to bring all this suffering upon himself. Three of them came by to share his grief and console him, sitting with him in silence for seven days. (Often, the ministry of presence is more powerful than any words.)

It would have been good if they had simply prayed for him and left, but instead they began to analyze his situation. Most of the book, from chapter 4 through chapter 37, consists of a dialogue between these three friends and Job. One friend summed up their argument by asking a pointed question: "Who, being innocent, has ever perished? Where were the upright ever destroyed?" (Job 4:7). In other words, they were convinced that Job was having a hard time because of a secret sin he needed to confess and forsake. That idea was the conventional wisdom of the day, and in some ways it is still at work today.

Job knew that he was not perfect, but he also knew that he had not done enough wrong to deserve all his troubles. He even affirmed his steadfast faith saying, "Though he slay me, yet will I hope in him" (Job 13:15). Then he proclaimed his faith in the afterlife with, "I know that my Redeemer lives, and that in the end he will stand upon the earth. And after my skin has been destroyed, yet in my flesh I will see God" (Job 19:25–26).

Throughout all of the arguing with his friends (and with God), Job failed to find a satisfactory explanation for his suffering. We never do. Weary of defending himself and at his wit's end, he eventually stopped arguing and listened to God.

When God finally broke the silence, he asked Job seventy or more questions that exposed Job's ignorance of God's greatness. He could not understand even the most common things like snow and ice, wind and rain, hail and lightning. He didn't understand how the world hangs on nothing in the vast expanse of space. He could not comprehend the ways of animals. The proud and rebellious Job is finally awed to silence, repenting and expressing faith in a God who is beyond him. He is finally content with the knowledge that he has fellowship with God and that he can be trusted. Bible scholar Charles Ryrie explains it this way:

> This is the great lesson of the book: If we know God, we do not need to know why he allows us to experience what we do. He is not only in control of the universe and its facets but also of our lives and he loves us. Though his ways are sometimes beyond our comprehension, we should not criticize him for his dealings with us or with others. God is always in control of all things, even when he appears not to be.[1]

In the end, God vindicates his servant Job by restoring his family with the birth of ten more children. He restores his wealth twofold, and he enjoys a long full life. The story closes, "The Lord blessed the latter part of Job's life more than the first . . ." (Job 42:12).

Job was no passive sufferer. He asked for answers passionately and persistently. He refused to accept the silence of God or the clichés of friends as answers. He was neither quiet nor pious in his pain. When he came to the end of his agony, he discovered that God did not *give* him an answer. God *is* the answer—his presence, power, and strength. As Job humbled himself before an all-wise and all-powerful God, he found peace and eventually restoration.

The message to us is that the age-old question of evil and suffering cannot be answered by philosophical arguments. No philosopher can heal the hurt or explain the agony and mystery of suffering. Only God can do that. Not many stories will have such a happy ending as Job's, but still there are lessons we need to learn from his struggles.

For example, we cannot plan for every calamity. We can only deepen our faith in God so that when tragedy strikes we will be prepared. Mike Tyson, the heavyweight boxer, once replied to those advising him before a fight, "Everyone has a plan until they get punched in the mouth."[2] What do you do when life punches you in the mouth and trouble strikes? Let me suggest these seven principles that may help you:

- Don't expect God to shield you from trouble just because you're his child.
- Don't blame God for everything that happens.
- It is not right to accept good from God and then complain about adversity.

- Guard against becoming bitter and angry with God when troubles come.
- Don't expect to understand everything that happens in life.
- Remember that no one knows the quality of his faith until it has been tested.
- Keep trusting God even when you don't understand what is happening to you or why it is happening.

No Exceptions and No Explanations

First, don't expect God to shield you from trouble just because you're his child. Satan accused God of building a hedge around Job to protect him, claiming that's why Job served him. Take away the hedge, Satan suggested, and Job's faith would crumble. That's when the testing started, and Job quickly learned that being one of God's children did not make him immune to life's difficulties.

The same is true for us. He never promises to spare us of problems but to strengthen us in them and to see us through them.

Why do bad things happen to good people? Let me answer that question up front. There are no good people. Jesus said there is only One who is good—God himself (Matthew 19:17). As Robert Louis Stevenson once wrote, "We all have feelings inside us that would shame hell." Some people may be better than others, but no one is without sin. No not one.

God promises no exemptions and no explanations for what happens in life. A quick review of Old Testament saints reveals that some of God's best people suffered most severely and unjustly—namely Joseph and Daniel. In the New Testament, the Apostle Paul, who poured out his life for the Lord, also suffered beatings, shipwrecks, scourging, and imprisonment when his only crime was preaching the gospel. The supreme example is that the sinless Son of God died a cruel death on Calvary's cross for all of us.

The Scriptures teach that God marks the fall of every sparrow. Jesus did not say that God keeps the sparrows from falling, just that he knows when they fall. Tragic things do happen that are unexplainable to our spirits, but we must be content with the knowledge that God knows and that God cares.

Give the Devil His Due 

Second, don't blame God for everything that happens. It was Satan who brought adversity into Job's life, not God. To blame God for everything is to blame him for evil and sin.

We live in a fallen world with Satan as its god (2 Corinthians 4:4). When man sinned, physical nature as well as human nature fell. No part of the world was untouched by sin. The Scriptures say that all creation "has been groaning as in the pains of childbirth" (Romans 8:22). What began as a glorious creation became a groaning creation because of sin.

Wars, cruelty, earthquakes, tornados—these were not a part of God's original design. They grew out of the rebellious spirit that dares to take apart the universe and put it back together in ways that will not work. These things are but the groans of nature longing for redemption.

When Jesus encountered a woman who had been sick and crippled for eighteen long years, he described her as one "whom Satan has kept bound" (Luke 13:16). Satan—not God.

The Apostle Paul had a painful bodily affliction that he called "a thorn in the flesh." He said it was a messenger *from Satan* to keep him beaten down (2 Corinthians 12:7). It was Satan—not God—who did it.

God is not in the business of hurting people. He is not the author of sickness, disaster, or death. Never once did he encounter a person who was sick or dying and say, "I'm sorry, my friend. It is God's will for you to suffer." He treated these ailments as intruders and aliens to God's universe.

The next time calamity strikes, instead of asking why God has done this to you, ask, "Why has the devil done this to me?"

Is God the Culprit? 

The third principle for understanding suffering involves realizing that it is not right to accept good from God and then complain about adversity. That was Job's answer to his wife's foolish suggestion to curse God and die as a result of their tragedies. Some insurance companies write policies that exclude certain "acts of God," presuming if something bad happens that you can't explain or don't expect, then God is the culprit. God becomes the whipping boy when there is no one else to whip. I once came across an insightful article by Bob Hastings about how God gets blamed for tornados and earthquakes, but not for sunshine and green hillsides.

In other words, life is a combination of good and bad. It is pure foolishness to accept good from God but complain about the least adversity that comes our way. Although we rejoice when God blesses us, the hard times he allows us to experience can also be a means of teaching and refining us. Reaching maturity in the faith means learning to accept both as part of life. God is in the rain and in the rainbow. Besides, all sunshine and no rain makes for a desert.

Keep Your Guard Up 

The fourth principle that will help us deal with hardship is to guard against becoming bitter and angry with God when troubles come. Remember that a pearl begins with the pain in the oyster's belly. Our great God is not obligated to make us comfortable. His goal is to conform us to the image of his Son, Jesus Christ, and sometimes he must use adversity to accomplish that.

I heard a story Billy Graham once shared about a friend who lost his job, his wife, and his home. But he held tenaciously to his faith—the only thing he had left. One day he stopped to watch some workmen installing stonework on a huge cathedral. One of them was chiseling a triangular piece of stone. "What are you doing with that?" asked Graham's friend. The workman pointed upwards and said, "See that little opening up there near the spire? I'm shaping this down here so that it will fit up there."

To the friend, it was as though God had spoken to his heart about the ordeal he was currently experiencing. "I'm shaping you down here so that you will fit up there."

God is not simply interested in saving souls. He also wants to build Christian character in our lives. Virtue is not something we inherit; it is something we build. French physician Alexis Carrel once observed that man is "both marble and sculptor."[3] Meaning, the way we respond to trials and trouble both builds and reveals character. In fact, the Greek word from which we get our word "character" means "a tool for engraving."

The Apostle Paul once wrote, "For our light and momentary troubles are achieving for us an eternal glory that far outweighs them all" (2 Cor. 4:17). If you're going through a hard time, hang in there! Maybe God is in the process of shaping you into exactly the person he wants you to be.

His Ways Versus Our Ways 

The fifth principle of managing hardship is not to expect to understand everything that happens in life. Augustine once wrote, "The Almighty does nothing without reason, though the frail of mind cannot always explain the reason." Just because things do not make sense *to us* does not mean that they don't make any sense *at all*.

One of the ironies of British history surrounds the end of World War II. Great Britain was victorious largely because of the courage, vision, and persistence of Prime Minister Winston Churchill. However, less than two months after VE Day, the country voted him out of office.

Churchill was understandably hurt. He even said of that event, "On the night of the 10th May 1940, at the outset of the mighty battle of Britain, I acquired the chief power in state, which henceforth I wielded in every-growing measure for five years and three months of world war, and at the end of which time, all of our enemies having surrendered unconditionally or being about to do so, I was immediately dismissed by the British electorate for all further conduct of their affairs."

When his wife told him, "Perhaps it is a blessing in disguise," Churchill replied, "It appears to be very effectively disguised." And so it often is when troubles come into our lives.

At that point, we simply fall back on the promises of God,

> "For my thoughts are not your thoughts, neither are your ways my ways," declares the LORD. "As the heavens are higher than the earth, so are my ways higher than your ways and my thoughts than your thoughts" (Isaiah 55:8–9).

Is Our Faith Real? 

The sixth principle we must remember when suffering is that no one knows the quality of his faith until it has been tested. Without adversity, people hardly know if they are honest or not. During hardship, we realize that life is a battleground, not a playground. We can't quit and go home crying to our mommas.

Joseph was another one of the sterling characters of the Old Testament. The Bible never mentions his faults, yet he suffered more than his share of setbacks. His jealous brothers sold him into slavery. The wife of his boss falsely accused him when he rejected her sexual advances. Then he was cast into prison for thirteen long years. Even in prison, the people he had befriended forgot him. He had every reason to become bitter, angry, and resentful. But he had a firm grip on the providence of God, and he would not allow this to happen. He learned rather than lamented.

When he confronted the brothers who had sold him into slavery, they feared his wrath. But Joseph said to them, "Don't be afraid. Am I in the place of God? You intended to harm me, but God intended it for good to accomplish what is now being done, the saving of many lives" (Genesis 50:19–20). Even God's Son "learned obedience from what he suffered" (Hebrews 5:8). Only a tested faith is a trusted faith.

When the Foundations Shake 

The final principle is to keep trusting God even when you don't understand what is happening or why. Remember, Job never knew why his troubles came, yet he vowed to trust God no matter what (Job 13:15).

Likewise, we need the faith of the three Hebrew children who were cast into the fiery furnace. They boldly claimed that God was able to deliver them—and even if he chose not to do so, they would continue to trust him (Daniel 3:17–18).

We need the faith of Habakkuk who promised to trust God even though everything else in his life failed (Habakkuk 3:17–19). Even if the stock market crashes, the oil patch dries up, the real estate market goes bust, and the bottom falls out, still we will trust the Lord.

Someone has said, "Sometimes we turn to God when our foundations are shaking, only to find out it is God who is shaking them." Understand this: nothing is final until God is finished. God deals in commas, not in periods. It's not over until it's over.

When I was growing up, neighborhood kids used to take turns watching baseball games through a knothole in the fence. It wasn't a very good view, but it was free. Our problem is that we have a knothole's view of life—we do not see the bigger picture. What God does, he does not always do overnight or according to our timetable. Sometimes even silence is the voice of God to us.

These answers may not fully satisfy, but they should help when life "smacks you in the mouth" and turns your plans upside down. Albert Einstein is often credited with saying, "Adversity introduces a man to himself." We hardly know ourselves until we have gone through hard times. It is God's way to bring triumph out of tragedy for those who trust in him. He did it with Job, and he can do it with you and me.

NOTES

1. Charles Ryrie, *Charles Ryrie Study Bible* (Chicago, IL: Moody Publishers, 2012), footnote 42:1–6.
2. http://articles.sun-sentinel.com/2012-11-09/sports/sfl-mike-tyson-explains-one-of-his-most-famous-quotes-20121109_1_mike-tyson-undisputed-truth-famous-quotes. Accessed 12/15/15.
3. Alexis Carrel, *Man, the Unknown* (Garden City, NY: Halcyon House, 1935).

One would think that the older we get,
the fewer worries we'd have.
The opposite is often true.
The longer we live, the more
we have to worry about.
We never outgrow the need for
Jesus' admonition not to worry.

6

Trust the Lord and Don't Worry

Matthew 6:25–34

Worry is one of the great enemies in the world today. I heard about a man who worried all the time, so much so that his friends were worried about him. Then one day they saw him walking down the street with a smile on his face, a spring in his step, and a whistle on his lips. Astonished, his buddies asked him, "What in the world has happened to you?" He said, "I hired somebody to do my worrying for me."

They responded, "How much did it cost you?"

The man replied, "$10,000."

"Where in the world are you going to get $10,000?" they wanted to know.

He just smiled and said, "That's his worry."

Many people's complaints fall into five categories. They feel they are overworked, overdrawn, overweight, overlooked, overwhelmed—or some combination thereof. Somehow we must find a way to deal with worry.

A man once told me, "Don't tell me worrying doesn't work. None of the things I worried about happened." That's the way it most often is. Most of what we worry about never comes to pass. So why worry in the first place?

Archbishop Trench was one of the great New Testament scholars whose work *Synonyms of the New Testament* is considered a classic. However, he developed an irrational fear that he would somehow lose all feeling in his limbs. The story is told that one night at an elaborate dinner he blurted out, "It finally happened! I haven't got a bit of feeling in my right leg." At that, the lady sitting next to him said, "Your Grace, if it will be any comfort to you, it's my leg you are pinching!"

An unknown poet said this of worry:

> Worry never climbed a hill
> Worry never paid a bill
> Worry never dried a tear
> Worry never calmed a fear
> Worry never darned a heel
> Worry never cooked a meal

It never led a horse to water
Nor ever did a thing it "oughter."

Worry is like a rocking chair, it's been said. It gives you something to do, but it doesn't get you anywhere. It is obviously a major problem because the Bible says so much about it. In fact, five times in the Sermon on the Mount, Jesus said not to worry, followed by a reason describing the futility of worry. The people listening to his sermon were like most of the world today: under-fed and under-clothed. While we are not in that same condition, we still manage to worry. Jesus said,

> Therefore I tell you, do not worry about your life, what you will eat or drink; or about your body, what you will wear. Is not life more important than food, and the body more important than clothes? (Matthew 6:25).

By worry, Jesus means don't be anxious, tense, or uptight. He is not saying we should not plan ahead or anticipate the future. He is simply saying we should not let it overwhelm us. In the Sermon on the Mount, Jesus gives us five things we should *not do* whenever we are tempted to worry:

- Don't undervalue yourself.
- Don't waste your time on what you can't change.
- Don't overlook the obvious.
- Don't act like a heathen.
- Don't borrow on tomorrow.

A Bird's-Eye View 

First, don't undervalue yourself when you are tempted to worry. Jesus said, "Look at the birds of the air; they do not sow or reap or store away in barns, and yet your heavenly Father feeds them. Are you not much more valuable than they?" (Matt. 6:26). In order to help us overcome the temptation to worry, Jesus stressed our value in God's eyes by pointing to the birds, one of the most common creations. If God cares for them, surely he will care for those who are made in his likeness.

This is not the only time that Jesus uses birds to teach us how much God values us. On another occasion Jesus said,

> Are not two sparrows sold for a penny? Yet not one of them will fall to the ground apart from the will of your Father. And even the very hairs of your head are all numbered. So don't be afraid; you are worth more than many sparrows (Matt. 10:29–31).

He chose the lowly, almost worthless sparrow to demonstrate his love and care. He did not point to the stately eagles that soar high in the sky, the graceful swans, or the singing nightingales. God attends the funeral of every sparrow. If he is that attentive to the birds, how much more is he concerned about us? If you take a bird's-eye view of life, you'll see that we have a caring heavenly Father.

The average man has about 100,000 hairs on his head. Yet as insignificant as a single hair is, God knows about it. Jesus is simply reminding us that there is so much more to life. We are eternal souls of enormous value in the sight of God. Remembering this first truth can eliminate a lot of worry, but Jesus has a lot more to say on the subject.

Water under the Bridge 

The second key to avoiding worry is not to waste your time on what you can't change. Jesus asked, "Who of you by worrying can add a single hour to his life?" (Matt. 6:27). The King James Version asks if worry can do so much as add one inch to your stature. It doesn't matter whether you're talking about inches or hours—worry cannot add either one to our lives. So why worry about what we cannot change?

Life is like water flowing under a bridge; once it is gone, it cannot be recalled. We need to learn to face our troubles honestly, do what we can about them, and realize that they are as water under a bridge.

In a Charlie Brown cartoon, Linus tells Charlie, "I guess it's wrong to always be worrying about tomorrow. Maybe we should think only about today." Charlie replies, "No, that's giving up. I'm still hoping that yesterday will get better."

The two greatest enemies of today are regrets about yesterday and fears about tomorrow. Yesterday has passed, and we cannot do anything about it unless there is an error we need to correct or someone with whom we must reconcile. The wise American humorist, Will Rogers, once cautioned, "Don't let yesterday use up too much of today."[1] Consider also the wisdom in this British nursery rhyme:

> For every evil under the sun,
> There is a remedy or there is none.
> If there is one, try to find it,
> If there is none, never mind it.[2]

What's the use about worrying about what you cannot change? Worry doesn't empty the day of its problems, only its strengths.

Practical Atheism 

The third instruction Jesus gives about worry is not to overlook the obvious. In other words, be sure to notice the flowers around you. Jesus said,

> And why do you worry about clothes? See how the flowers of the field grow. They do not labor or spin. Yet I tell you that not even Solomon in all his splendor was dressed like one of these. If that is how God clothes the grass of the field, which is here today and tomorrow is thrown into the fire,

> will he not much more clothe you, O you of little faith? (Matt. 6:28–30).

In a sense, worry is a form of atheism; it is a denial of God's concern and of Christ's intercessory work. If you doubt God's concern, just look around you. The flowers of the field indicate his loving care. He compares their beauty to Solomon, the King of Israel and one of the wealthiest men who ever lived.

When the Queen of Sheba came to see this wealth she heard so much about, she exclaimed that the half had not been told to her. Solomon had 40,000 stalls of horses, and his guards carried shields of pure gold. The temple he built for God contained today's equivalent of five billion dollars in silver and gold. It took 157,000 workmen five-and-a-half years to complete it. Yet with all of his power and wealth, God says he was not arrayed more beautifully than the common flowers of the field. If you don't overlook the obvious around you, you'll see how God can take care of you.

If atheism is at the root of worry, then faith is the answer. The Apostle Paul shared the antidote for worry,

> Do not be anxious about anything, but in every situation, by prayer and petition, with thanksgiving, present your requests to God. And the peace of God, which transcends all understanding, will guard your hearts and your minds in Christ Jesus (Philippians 4:6–7).

His advice is simple: Don't worry about anything. Pray about everything and be thankful in all things, and you will have peace. Isaiah writes, "You will keep in perfect peace him whose mind is steadfast, because he trusts in you" (Isaiah 26:3).

Watch Out for a Divided Mind

If we want to work on our tendency to worry, we must follow the fourth principle we find in this passage. Jesus warns against acting like those who do not know God. Jesus said,

> So do not worry, saying, 'What shall we eat?' or 'What shall we drink?' or 'What shall we wear?' For the pagans run after all these things, and your heavenly Father knows that you need them. But seek first his kingdom and his righteousness, and all these things will be given to you as well (Matt. 6:31–33).

Jesus is saying don't act like the heathen. Keep your priorities in order, and seek the kingdom of God first.

Our English word "worry" comes from the Greek word "merimnao." It is a combination of "to divide" and "mind." Therefore, worry means "to divide the mind." It divides our mind between the kingdoms of this world and the kingdom of God, and takes us away from the things of God.

Martha demonstrated a classic example of a divided mind when Jesus visited their home in Bethany. It was one of those rare occasions when he sat down to talk one-on-one. Her sister Mary sat down at his feet and listened to his teachings. But Martha was distracted, busily trying to prepare an elaborate meal for Jesus. She soon became anxious and showed Jesus how perturbed she was that Mary was not helping her.

> "Martha, Martha," the Lord answered, "you are worried and upset about many things, but only one thing is needed. Mary has chosen what is better, and it will not be taken away from her" (Luke 10:41–42).

He fussed at her about her fussiness. Martha's primary concern was preparing a meal that would last only a little while. Mary's concern was to listen to his words that would endure forever.

The answer to a divided mind is to focus your attention on Jesus Christ and to seek his kingdom above everything else. A divided mind makes mountains out of molehills. One way to test your memory is to try to remember all the things that you worried about yesterday.

One Day at a Time 

Finally, Jesus tells us not to borrow on tomorrow. "Therefore do not worry about tomorrow, for tomorrow will worry about itself. Each day has enough trouble of its own" (Matt. 6:34). Jesus is telling us to live one day at a time. If we live each day for God's glory, we will automatically be prepared for tomorrow.

Scottish philosopher Thomas Carlyle had a great mind, but he used to get terribly upset over trifling matters. It is said that his neighbor's rooster crowed very early in the morning. "Does the crowing keep you awake?" his neighbor asked when Carlyle complained.

"No, it's not the crowing that keeps me awake," Carlyle replied. "It's lying there expecting him to crow." That's what I call borrowing on tomorrow.

Explorer Sir Morton Stanley was once asked on an expedition if he had been frightened of the horrifying jungle that had daunted previous men. He said in reply, "I did not see the whole. I only saw this rock ahead of me; I only saw the poisonous snake which I had to kill in order to take the next step. I only saw the problem directly in front of me. If I had seen the whole thing, I would have been too overwhelmed to have attempted this."[3]

That's the way we must face life—one day at a time. I heard a story about a young medical student at Montreal General Hospital in 1871 named William Osler. Already worried about his final examinations, Osler grew increasingly troubled about what he should do with his life, where he should establish his medical practice, and how he would build it. Then he read twenty-one words penned by Thomas Carlyle that changed his outlook: "Our main business is not to see what is dimly at a distance, but to do what is clearly at hand."

Encouraged by this truth, Osler went on to establish his medical practice and eventually founded the famous Johns Hopkins School of Medicine. No wonder George MacDonald once wrote, "No man ever sank under the burden of the day. Only when tomorrow's burden is added to the burden of today that the weight is more than a man can bear. Never load yourself so."

Theologian Nels Ferré once shared about a dream his wife had. In the dream, she was sitting at a table having to write the answer to the question, "How can I quit worrying?" She wrote at great length, but upon waking she could only remember three words: worship, work, and wait. With those three words I think you can also find peace in life. Worship, seek the Lord in prayer; work, get busy helping someone else; wait, practice patience by giving God a chance to work. As the 18th century believer Jean-Pierre de Caussade wrote in *The Joy of the Saint*, "Leave the past to the infinite mercies of God; the future to his good providence; give the present wholly to his love by being faithful to his grace."

If all else fails and you find yourself worrying, look at the life of Jesus. He was never in a hurry. There was no rushing forward, no anticipating, no fretting over what might be. He fulfilled each day's duties as they came along, and the rest he left with God. We need to do the same.

NOTES

1. Earliest attribution to Will Rogers in *The Vocational Guidance Quarterly, Volumes 9–10* (National Career Development Association, 1960), 183.
2. John Newbery, ed., *Mother Goose's Melody* (London, England, 1765).
3. John McCarter and Joan Feeney, *Starting at the Top* (New York, NY: William Morrow & Co., 1985), quoted by Steven R. Covey, *Everyday Greatness: Inspiration for a Meaningful Life*, (Nashville, TN: Thomas Nelson, 2009), 325.

People of all ages fear outliving their income. That's just one reason to watch our money and be good stewards from the start.

7 Watch Your Money

Deuteronomy 6:10–12

In a time when people want to get rich quick, we need to remember the potential downside to prosperity. In a letter to American diplomat Adlai Stevenson, John Steinbeck wrote,

> A strange species we are. We can stand anything God and nature can throw at us save only plenty. If I wanted to destroy a nation, I would give it too

> much, and I would have it on its knees, greedy, and sick.[1]

Likewise, the late columnist James Reston is often credited as saying, "Americans have always been able to handle austerity and even adversity. Prosperity is what is doing us in."

We are not the first people to face the dangers of prosperity. Three thousand years ago, Moses gave a similar warning to the children of Israel.

> When the LORD your God brings you into the land he swore to your fathers, to Abraham, Isaac and Jacob, to give you—a land with large, flourishing cities you did not build, houses filled with all kinds of good things you did not provide, wells you did not dig, and vineyards and olive groves you did not plant—then when you eat and are satisfied, be careful that you do not forget the LORD, who brought you out of Egypt, out of the land of slavery (Deuteronomy 6:10–12).

That was not the only time he cautioned them about the downside of their future success. He repeated later,

> Be careful that you do not forget the LORD your God, failing to observe his commands, his laws and his decrees that I am giving you this day. Otherwise, when you eat and are satisfied, when

> you build fine houses and settle down, and when your herds and flocks grow large and your silver and gold increase and all you have is multiplied, then your heart will become proud and you will forget the LORD your God, who brought you out of Egypt, out of the land of slavery (Deut. 8:11–14).

Then he adds,

> You may say to yourself, 'My power and the strength of my hands have produced this wealth for me.' But remember the LORD your God, for it is he who gives you the ability to produce wealth . . . (Deut. 8:17–18).

The Lord knew the power that money can exact over people. Some scholars claim there are over 1,000 verses in the Bible dealing with financial issues. About 15% of what Jesus said was about money. In fact, he said more about wealth and material possessions than he did about heaven and hell. We need a healthy view of money in order to live the remainder of our lives for him.

You will succeed in stewarding your money if you will practice these three principles:

- Never use money as a measure of wealth.
- Don't confuse your net worth with your self-worth.
- Learn to let go of money before it grabs hold of you.

The Richest Man in Town

First, never use money as a measure of wealth. The movie *Broken Trails* starring Robert Duval is the story of an old man and his nephew who drive a herd of horses from Oregon to Wyoming to make money. Along the way, they end up rescuing five Chinese girls from the sex slave market, but this slows them down and threatens their payout. The old man says to his nephew, "This deal is getting more interesting by the day." The young man replies in frustration, "This deal is becoming less profitable by the day." But the wiser old man sees helping the girls as far more important than the money they could make and cautions him, "Son, don't ever use money as a measure of wealth."

Materialism is the belief that "things" are the supreme value in life. But the Scriptures keep reminding us that things are not what is most important. God and people are the most important, and there is more than one way to be rich. For example, you can have a wealth of friends and good memories. You can also be rich in good works.

Jim Denison tells an allegory about a rich man named Carl who often rode around his vast estate so he could congratulate himself on his great wealth. One day while riding, he saw Hans, an old tenant farmer known for his generosity to people in need. As he stopped to talk, Hans said to him, "It is strange that you should come by today, for I had a dream last night. A voice told me, 'The richest man in the valley will die tonight.' I don't know what it means, but I thought I should tell you."

Carl laughed it off and galloped away. But the old farmer's words troubled him because Carl was obviously the richest man in the valley. That evening he called his personal physician and told him what Hans had said. After a thorough examination, the doctor assured him he would not die that night and even offered to play cards all night with him just in case.

As dawn broke, Carl thanked the doctor and told him how foolish he felt for being upset by the old man's dream. Just then a messenger arrived at Carl's door to tell him that Hans had died that night in his sleep.[2]

The Bible reminds us,

> Command those who are rich in this present world not to be arrogant nor to put their hope in wealth, which is so uncertain, but to put their hope in God, who richly provides us with everything for our enjoyment. Command them to do good, to be rich in good deeds, and to be generous and willing to share (1 Timothy 6:17–18).

This world's currency has little value in God's sight, and a person can have personal wealth and not be rich toward God (Luke 12:21). Make sure you are wealthy in all that money cannot buy.

Don't Get Choked to Death 

If you want to manage your money better, you must also learn not to confuse your net worth with your self-worth. Bernice Washington, a high profile businesswoman, author, and motivational speaker became the highest-ranking woman of color in an international pharmaceutical company. She wrote a book *How to Ride Thunder and Catch Lightning: Success Principles from Father to Daughter* about what she learned from her sharecropper father. He told his five children that he was going to give them an opportunity to have a better life, adding that he would send each one to college once and get them out of jail once! He also taught them about showing gratitude to God for allowing them to live together as a family. When a classmate teased Bernice about being "poor" in junior high, it brought her to tears. Later that day at home, her father hugged her and explained, "Baby, we're not poor. We just don't have any money." That, she said, was a defining moment in her life.

Jesus spoke about the "deceitfulness of wealth" and its ability to choke the word of God out of our lives (Matthew 13:22). How is it deceitful? There are at least three ways that wealth can fool you. It can make you think that if you have it, you'll be happy; it can make you think if you have it, you will be secure; it can make you think that if you have it, you will be somebody important. However, none of these are true.

Wealth does not bring happiness. As Benjamin Franklin said, "Money never made a man happy yet, nor will it. The more a man has, the more he wants. Instead of filling a vacuum, it makes one." Money doesn't bring security either. Remember, the rich farmer who said one day he finally "had it made" died that same night (Luke 12:16–21).

Money cannot give you importance either. What is the value of a person? In the first century, a slave was worth two donkeys. The raw value of the fifty-four chemicals comprising an average-sized man is about $4.97. But these monetary values do not come close to the true worth of a person. Measure your value against the fact that you have been created in the image of God, redeemed by the Son of God, and filled by the Spirit of God. Never confuse the idea that your net worth and your self-worth are the same.

In a 1907 speech to McGill University students in Montreal, Canada, writer Rudyard Kipling urged students to not be concerned with money, position, and personal glory. He warned that one day they would meet a man who cares for none of these things, and then they would find out how poor they really were in comparison. Be rich toward God. That's true wealth.

Learning to Let Go 

The final truth is that we must learn to let go of our wealth before it grabs hold of us. Pastor Bill Leslie used to say that the Bible asks three main questions about money: (1) How did you get it? (legally/justly or exploitatively), (2) What are you doing with it? (indulging in luxuries or helping the needy), (3) What is it doing to you? Material items have a way of getting a grip on us. We start out possessing them, and they wind up possessing us. It's at that point that we learn, often too late, how money is a wonderful servant but a terrible master.

An anonymous prospector on the wild frontier scratched this final lament on the wall of his shack in Deadwood, South Dakota: "I lost my gun. I lost my horse. I'm out of food. The Indians are after me. But I've got all the gold I can carry."[3] We all have a kinship to that miner. It's just hard to let go.

In his book *How Much Land Does a Man Need?* Leo Tolstoy tells a similar story about an ambitious tenant farmer who is offered free all the land that he can encircle on foot in a day. After running at full speed for several hours, he acquires several square miles of valuable property. It is more soil than he could till in a lifetime and more than enough to make him and his family rich for generations.

The poor fellow, drenched with sweat and gasping for breath, thinks about stopping—for what's the point of going any further? But he can't help himself. He races ahead to maximize his opportunity until he drops dead of exhaustion just as the last rays of the sun fade from the sky. He started out to possess the land, and in the end it possessed him. It takes a mature person to handle wealth wisely. That may be why someone said, "People with wealth are not so much to be envied as to be prayed for."

Ernest Campbell, former pastor of New York's Riverside Church, once shared the following in a sermon:

> Many people now in the church are in the middle-income bracket. They got there not by dropping down from a higher bracket but by coming up from a lower. One of the hardest things to learn when you come up is to learn how to let go. I grew up in the Depression years. I recall my mother giving us those little envelopes every Sunday—five cents on one side and one cent on the other. That was about all we could spare at the time. When you grow up poor like that, you become imbued with what has been called the 'ethic of privation.' You feel that you had better hold on to what you have. The pity is that some of us have not matured. We are still in the taking stage and think that's all there is to the Christian life.

Then Campbell added:

> To be young is to study in schools that you did not build. To be mature is to build schools in which you will not study.
>
> To be young is to swim in pools you did not dig. To be mature is to dig pools in which you will not swim.
>
> To be young is to sit under trees you did not plant. To be mature is to plant trees under which you will not sit.

> To be young is to dance to music you did not write. To be mature is to write music to which you will not dance.
>
> To be young is to benefit from a church which you did not make. To be mature is to make a church from which you might not benefit.

Jesus said it is more blessed to give than to receive, but many of us miss the best in life because we hang on to what we've got. Thomas Carlyle tells about hearing a knock on the door of his home one day and finding a beggar asking for a handout. Without a thought he rushed upstairs, got his piggy bank with all his savings, cracked it open, and handed it all to the beggar. Then Carlyle said, "At that moment I felt more at home with who I am and why I am here. Sadly that's the last time I felt that way." I guess the older he got, the harder it was to let go. I suppose most of us face the same problem.

If a person is growing large in wealth, nothing but constant "letting go" and giving can keep him from growing small in his soul. We simply must learn to let go.

Learning to do this is also one way to enrich our earthly lives by accumulating wonderful memories. In one of the early *Downton Abbey* series television shows, the servant Mr. Bates described the purpose of life as accumulating good memories. The purpose of life is greater than that, but I agree that good memories result from a life spent sharing your wealth with others.

I have a friend who collects sports memorabilia. One day he showed me one of his prized possessions—a football signed by the great quarterback Sammy Baugh. After an all-American career at Texas Christian University, Baugh had an all-pro career with the Washington Redskins. He is credited with transforming the game by perfecting the forward pass and making it the primary offensive weapon in football. In his sixteen-year career, he was named all-pro six times and led the league in passing six times, in punting four times, and in interceptions once. After retiring, he returned to his ranch in West Texas where he lived until he moved into an assisted care home and died at the age of ninety-three.

According to my friend, while Baugh was in the assisted care home, a man visited him and asked how much he would charge to sign three footballs. Baugh told the man he charged $200 each and the man agreed. As he prepared to sign the balls, Baugh complained about the food and offered to sign the balls for free if the man went down the street and brought him a hamburger and a drink. The man jumped at the offer and got the food.

After he signed the balls, Baugh asked what the man would do with them. The man replied, "I'm going to sell them for $300 each." Baugh then cautioned that whatever profit he made would soon be gone. But, Baugh suggested, if he gave the balls away he would have good memories forever. My friend then pointed to his treasured football and said, "And that's how I got this one. The man gave it to me." If you are into collecting memories more that memorabilia, learn to let go and give generously . . . the memories last forever.

It is not a sin to have wealth, but it does bring enormous responsibility. At the end of your life, you'll be evaluated and rewarded according to how you handled what God entrusted to you. That includes your wealth, so watch it. You control it; don't let it control you. Remember you are worth more than you possess, and practice letting go for the good of others.

NOTES

1. John Steinbeck, quoted by Richard C. Halverson, *Perspective: Devotional Thoughts for Men* (Grand Rapids, MI: Zondervan Publishing House, 1987).
2. http://baptistwaypress.texasbaptists.org/files/2011/10/EzraHaggai-14.pdf. Accessed 1/20/16.
3. David Yount, *Celebrating the Rest of Your Life* (Minneapolis, MN: Augsburg Books, 2005), 153.

The older we become,
the more we value good
neighbors and the more we
need to work at being one.

8

Be a Good Neighbor

The four-year-old son of a pastor was deeply impressed with the stories he heard in Vacation Bible School one summer. One day he came home and told his dad, "There was this guy walking down the road. And these other three guys jumped on him, beat him up, and took all his money. Then two other guys came by and didn't even stop. But along came this good American. He put the man on his horse and carried him to Mexico."

Without skipping a beat, the boy then asked the question that all of us will ultimately have to answer: "Daddy, these Americans are the good guys, aren't they?"

If Jesus had been telling the story in our day, I think he might have spoken of a good American instead of a Good Samaritan! And he really might have been going to Mexico instead of Jericho, but the truth would be the same—be a good neighbor to anyone who is in need.

Consider again the timeless story of the Good Samaritan in Luke 10:25–37, and the context that came before it. Jesus was in the midst of a busy day of teaching when a student of the law of God asked him what he had to do to have eternal life. Jesus then asked him what the Scriptures said, and the man responded correctly—to love the Lord your God with all your heart, soul, strength, and mind, and to love your neighbor as yourself. Jesus commended his answer.

However, the man obviously was not keeping this command and, wishing to justify his failure, asked Jesus a second question. "Who is my neighbor?" he wanted to know, as if to say, "If I had only known who they were, I'd have done my duty." That was an urgent question among Jewish scholars. Yet they did nothing but discuss it. In order to take it out of the realm of theory and into practicality, Jesus told them a parable.

It was a story of a Jewish man going from Jerusalem to Jericho. The road between the two cities was notoriously dangerous. Jerusalem is 2,300 feet above sea level; the Dead Sea near Jericho is 1,300 feet below sea level. Dropping 3,600 feet in about twenty miles, the road carves and twists its way through rocks and crags, making it a hunting ground for thieves.

In the story, robbers attacked the man and stripped him of his clothing, beat him, and left him by the side of the road half-dead. In time, along came a Jewish priest (a religious officer), but he ignored this man's plight and simply passed by on the other side. Next, a Levite (another religious leader) also likewise ignored him. Finally, a Samaritan came upon the man and felt compassion for him. He bandaged up his wounds, carried the man on his donkey, and left him at an inn where they could take care of him at the Samaritan's expense.

Afterwards, Jesus asked, "Which of these three do you think was a neighbor to the man who fell into the hands of robbers?" The expert in the law then replied, "The one who had mercy on him." Jesus told him to "go and do likewise" (Luke 10:36–37). If you miss the part about "go and do likewise," you miss the punch line of the story.

With these words, Jesus elevated the Scriptures from "for-discussion-only" to everyday life. Obeying God is more than reciting a creed or observing a ceremony—it is a life we must live—a life of love for God and love for our neighbor.

Someone has said that this parable presents three philosophies of life. That of the robbers: "What's yours is mine, I'll take it!" That of the priests and Levites: "What's mine is mine, I'll keep it!" That of the Samaritan: "What's mine is yours, I'll share it!" I've also heard it said that the story presents three kinds of people—those who beat us up, those who pass us up, and those who help us up. I like how the missionary J. Ivey Miller described each kind: the hurting people of the world, the heartless people of the world, and the helpful people of the world.

Regardless of how you break it down, the simple truth of this parable is that anybody who is in need is our neighbor. The charge and challenge of the story is to go and do like this Samaritan. Underscore those words in your mind. Repeat them to yourself. Memorize them, and most of all, practice them. For as long as the world stands, as long as God gives us breath, we are commanded to go and imitate him.

In order to be a good neighbor, I must help people in need . . .

- Regardless of who is in need.
- Regardless of the inconvenience.
- Regardless of what others do.

Be Compassionate

The first truth is that we should "go and do" like this Samaritan, regardless of who is in need. We miss the barb of this parable if we don't understand first century Jewish and Samaritan relationships. It was the most acute racial, national, and religious issue of that day, for the Jews had no dealings with the Samaritans (John 4:9).

The Samaritans were considered half-breeds, the result of intermarriage between Jews and Assyrians. They had their own form and place of worship apart from the Jews.

So intense was their hatred of one another, the Jews often referred to Samaritans as "dogs," and if it could be avoided, they would not even walk through the region of Samaria.

Ironically, Jesus makes a Samaritan the hero of this story. He never did anything by accident, so he was emphasizing our responsibility to reach out and help people no matter who they are. There are no social, racial, national, or cultural boundaries to block off a Christian's neighborhood. We are to help any person, anywhere, under any circumstance.

Another story in the Bible illustrates the amazing openness of Jesus. Remember the woman at the well in Samaria? She was of questionable reputation, ostracized by her own people. When Jesus spoke to her she was astonished, as were the disciples, at his inclusiveness. First, they were shocked that he spoke to a woman at all. Men simply did not speak to women in public, not even their wives. Certainly no rabbi would speak to a woman in public. More than that, this was a Samaritan woman who had been married and divorced five times and now had a live-in boyfriend.

But Jesus was not, and is not, bound by our stereotypes. He will have nothing to do with attitudes that might restrict our openness to others, and he demonstrated this truth repeatedly. Once when he needed to make a quick trip to Jerusalem he decided to take a shortcut through Samaria, rather than take the long way around it. He sent his disciples ahead to arrange for food and lodging, and when the Samaritans were unwelcoming, James and John wanted to call down fire down from heaven and destroy them (Luke 9:54). They had good scriptural precedence for this idea. Elijah had done the same to a group of soldiers from Moab who had come to arrest him (2 Kings 1:14). Jesus reproved their attitude, saying that he came to save the world—even the Samaritans—and not to destroy it.

Then there was the time when a group of ten lepers, Jews and Samaritans alike, begged Jesus to heal them. Suffering can make for strange bedfellows like little else. Jesus did heal all the men, but only one returned to give thanks—a Samaritan (Luke 17:11–19).

Jesus also opened his heart and his life to tax collectors like Zacchaeus, to lepers like Simon, and to women of questionable reputation like Mary. He welcomed all people and so should we. Dr. Jeff Ray, who once taught at Southwestern Seminary, frequently told his students, "Be kind to everybody because everybody is having a hard time." Ours is a needy world, and the road of life is littered with fallen brothers and sisters. Don't pass them up when you can lift them up.

The late Hubert H. Humphrey, who served as Vice President of the United States under Lyndon Johnson, once described the measure of a society by how its members treat those in the sunrise of life (children), those in the sunset of life (elderly), and those in the shadows of life (the sick and dying). To that I would add a fourth category: those in the gutters of life. Those who are down and out, even if it is the result of their own doing. There are no disposable people. As George W. Carver said, "Be kind to others. How far you go in life depends on being tender with the young, compassionate with the aged, sympathetic with the striving, tolerant of the weak and the strong. Because someday in life you will have been all of these."[1]

If we are to "go and do likewise" regardless of who is in need, we must incorporate a three-pronged approach. First, we must be aware of them. We are often so caught up in ourselves that we are unaware of hurting people around us. Second, we must care for them. We must put our love into action, reach out, and help them by showing the love of Christ in concrete ways. Third, we must share with them God's love. We live in a big neighborhood; it's as wide as the world. Everyone, regardless of who they are, is our neighbor.

Don't Stop and Count the Cost

The second principle involved in being a good neighbor is to do so regardless of the inconvenience. Being a good neighbor can be expensive. It can cost you money. More than that, it can cost time, emotional energy, patience, disappointment, and heartache because we never know how our acts of kindness will turn out.

While we think of "cost" primarily in terms of money, the needs of most people cannot be met with money alone. Mother Teresa observed,

> The greatest disease in the world today is not TB or leprosy; it is being unwanted, unloved, and uncared for. We can cure physical diseases with medicine, but the only cure for loneliness, despair and hopelessness is love. There are many in the world who are dying for a piece of bread, but there

> are more dying for a little love. The poverty in the West is a different kind of poverty—it is not only a poverty of loneliness, but of spirituality. There's a hunger for love, and there is a hunger for God.[2]

It was widely reported when the late Johnny Carson, longtime host of NBC's *The Tonight Show*, returned to his hometown of Norfolk, Nebraska, to attend a dinner honoring his favorite teacher, Faye Gordon. For years, Carson had told Miss Gordon he would visit her on her 100th birthday. He stayed true to his word, though his arrival at her nursing home was a surprise for her. The event included a serenade, an old-fashioned farm dinner of pan-fried chicken, and talk of the woman's long life. Carson praised Miss Gordon for the contribution she made to his life and the lives of her other students. He also gave her a music box that played *Unforgettable*, but Miss Gordon described her real gift as the visit itself.

Most of the world's hurts cannot be met with money, only with compassion. We need a servant's heart that doesn't simply stop and stare but stoops and shares. A visit, a call, or a note may be enough. Today, we think of a philanthropist as someone who donates big sums of money, yet the word is derived from two Greek words: "philos" (loving) and "anthropos" (man). It translates to "loving man." All of us are capable of being philanthropists in that sense. We can give ourselves to others.

Likewise, we need the servant heart of the Apostle Paul. When the ship he was on sank off the coast of Malta, he gathered brushwood for a fire to warm the cold, wet survivors. He had to be just as exhausted everyone else, but he did what everyone needed. No task is beneath you if you have a servant's heart.

One of the problems with trying to help people with physical and emotional needs is that we must help them on their terms—when, where, and how they are hurting. We can't wait until it is a convenient time for us. Unfortunately, many of God's people have lost that servant spirit, including ministers. Pastor Rick Warren even wrote, "Many leaders start out as servants and end up as celebrities. They become addicted to attention, unaware that always being in the limelight blinds you."[3] Perhaps that's why the priest and the Levite walked by on the other side of the road. They were blinded by their prejudices and their positions and maybe even their pressing duties.

Selfishness is self-destruction in slow motion. When we close our eyes to others, unwilling to get involved and pay the price to help them, we die a little bit ourselves. Once again, Mother Teresa said it best, "We can do no great things, only small things with great love." That's what the world needs.

I Have Done Nothing— And of That I Am Ashamed

The third truth is that we should go and do like this Good Samaritan regardless of what others do. The Samaritan could have easily excused himself, saying, "His fellow countrymen did not help him, why should I?" But he didn't do that. He knew that the failures of others did not excuse him.

Inside the Holocaust Memorial Museum in Washington D.C. are these words: "Thou shalt not be a victim. Thou shalt not be a perpetrator. Above all, thou shalt not be a bystander." In the movie *The Patriot* Mel Gibson plays a peaceful farmer before the murder of his son eventually pulls him into the American Revolution. In one scene, he expresses grief over his hesitation to get involved. When someone assures him he has done nothing of which to be ashamed, Gibson simply replies, "I have done nothing—and of that I am ashamed." We can never excuse ourselves because others do not do all that they should. You can't lift everyone, but you can lift someone.

If we're going to be fully alive, we have to help others. You're going to give your life to something. What will it be—a career, a sport, a hobby, fame, wealth? None of these has lasting significance. Service is the best way to attain real significance.

Once again, Rick Warren reminds us,

> If you are not involved in any service or ministry, what excuse have you been using? Abraham was old, Jacob was insecure, Leah was unattractive, Joseph was abused, Moses stuttered, Gideon was poor, Samson was codependent, Rahab was immoral, David had an affair and all kinds of family problems, Elijah was suicidal, Jeremiah was depressed, Jonah was reluctant, Naomi was

> a widow, John the Baptist was eccentric to say the least, Peter was impulsive and hot tempered, Martha worried a lot, the Samaritan woman had several failed marriages, Zacchaeus was unpopular, Thomas had doubts, Paul had poor health, and Timothy was timid. That's quite a variety of misfits, but God used each of them in his service. And he will use you too if you'll stop making excuses.[4]

Mickey Mantle came to the end of his life as perhaps the greatest baseball player ever—but he wasted his life on alcohol. He admitted, "God gave me a great body and the ability to play baseball . . . God gave me everything and I just . . . pfttt!"[5] When asked how he would like to be remembered, he gave this unvarnished plea: "I'd like to say to kids out there, if you're looking for a role model, don't look at me." A reporter once asked Mantle, who had received a liver transplant, if he had signed a donor card. "Everything I've got is worn out," he said. "Although I've heard people say they would like to have my heart . . . it's never been used." What a tragic end to a great talent. God gave us all a heart to be aware, to care, and to share.

Theodore Roosevelt, the 26th president of the United States, claimed this motto for his life:

> Look up, not down
> Look out, not in
> Look forward, not backward
> And lend a hand[6]

That's what it means to be a good American—and a good Samaritan.

NOTES

1. http://www.nps.gov/nr/travel/cultural_diversity/G_Washington_Carver_Historic_Site.html. Accessed 12/29/15.
2. Mother Teresa, *A Simple Path* (New York, NY: Ballantine Books, 1995), 79.
3. Rick Warren, *The Purpose Driven Life* (Grand Rapids, MI: Zondervan Publishing House, 2002), 263.
4. http://rickwarren.org/devotional/english/what-excuse-have-you-been-using. Accessed 1/3/16.
5. Jane Leavey, *The Last Boy: Mickey Mantle and the End of America's Childhood* (New York, NY: Harper Perennial, 2011), 374.
6. David McCollough, *Mornings on Horseback: The Story of an Extraordinary Family, a Vanished Way of Life and the Unique Child Who Became Theodore Roosevelt* (New York, NY: Simon & Schuster, 1982), 197.

When we are young, we are usually too busy living to struggle with knowing who we are and why we are here. But before the last leaf falls, we need to know the truth.

9

Know Who You Are

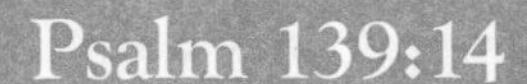

Acting legend Kirk Douglas was driving to Palm Springs, California one day when he stopped to give a sailor a lift. The serviceman seemed to recognize something vaguely familiar, especially the driver's blue eyes and famous dimple on his chin. He then said to Douglas, "Hey! Do you know who you are?"

Douglas, in an interview with a *Chicago Tribune* writer, said that question was what inspired him to find out who he was, put the pieces together, and "see what . . . comes out."[1] He had to explore where he came from, what he had come through, and what he had come to.

In his autobiography *The Ragman's Son*, Douglas writes that he was born the only son of illiterate Russian Jews.[2] He had a love-hate relationship with his father, a ragman and a drunk, who never affirmed him or offered a pat on the back his entire life. His is a story full of pain and anger, leaving him feeling like "nobody" most of his life. In fact, it was his own unhappiness that led him to analyze his life, starting with that question, "Do you know who you are?"

That question is one we all need to ask ourselves. To find the answer, we also need to know where we came from, what we we've come through, and where we have come to. The first question has to do with your ancestors. Where did you come *from*? It's important to know who your parents were. I have read that many adopted children have an identity crisis because they want to know their birth parents. They don't want to live with them, but they want to know about them and why they chose adoption. Knowing your parents and remembering key things that important people said to you early in life all help to define who you are. Maya Angelou once said, "I've learned that people will forget what you've said. People will forget what you did. But people will never forget how you made them feel." What people said to me as I was growing up, especially encouraging words, helped to shape my life even today.

The second question has to do with your life's experiences. What have you come *through*? Novelist Aldous Huxley wisely noted, "Experience is not what happens to you. It is what you do with what happens to you." All that we have experienced up until today has molded us into who we really are.

The final question is this: What we have come *to*? This question has to do with what we have made of ourselves and whether we consider ourselves a success or failure in our chosen field. Try as we may, we can never escape these issues—where we came from, what we've come through, and what we have come to.

As I mentioned in a previous chapter, William Wilberforce contemplated giving up politics but chose to serve Christ in the political arena. Before he converted, he was a typical partisan politician. After his conversion, he did his best to serve as a Christian statesman, although it was a role for which he had no sure pattern. Nevertheless, his transformation was remarkable, and the course of his life was forever altered. Renouncing the win-at-all-cost politics of hostility and vehemence, many contemporaries and political opponents said he came to exhibit a good faith even in people with whom he had strong differences.

Over time, Wilberforce also exemplified a civility that had been glaringly absent. Frances Bacon, the 16th century essayist Wilberforce much admired, once commented, "It's a sad fate for a man to be so well known to everybody else, and still unknown to himself." Wilberforce had finally found his rest and peace with God.[3]

When I read that statement by Bacon—well known to everybody else and still unknown to himself—it captured my attention. It brought me back to, "Hey! Do you know who you are?" You can explore the details of where you came from, what you've come through, and what you've come to on your own. This chapter takes a broader approach to remind you of the person you really are. We'll focus on three truths:

- You are an original, not a copy.
- You are not your past.
- You are not made for time but for eternity.

Be Yourself 

First, you are not a copy. You are an original. The Scriptures remind us that we are "fearfully and wonderfully made" (Psalm 139:14). The psalmist goes on to say that God not only created us but also knows our every thought and act. We are continually on his mind, the unique creation of God.

A sign outside a middle school in New Ipswich, New Hampshire, once read, "You are unique—just like everyone else." Yet the fact is, you are! The Apostle Paul puts it this way, "For we are God's handiwork, created in Christ Jesus to do good works, which God prepared in advance for us to do" (Ephesians 2:10). Our English word "poem" comes from the Greek translation "workmanship." Rick Warren writes,

> You are God's handcrafted work of art. You are not an assembly-line product, mass produced without thought. You are a custom-designed, one-of-a-kind, original masterpiece.[4]

In *The Purpose Driven Life*, Warren goes on to define what an amazing creature you are.

> For instance, your brain can store 100,000,000,000,000 facts. Your mind can handle 15,000 decisions a second, as is the case when your digestive system is working. Your nose can smell up to 10,000 different odors. Your touch can detect an item 1/25,000th of an inch thick. Your tongue can taste one part of quinine in 2 million parts of water. You're a bundle of incredible abilities, an amazing creation of God.[5]

To that I would add that your skin replaces itself every thirty days. And the lining of your stomach replaces itself every seven days. Nothing that gets in your mind ever gets out. I'm in my eighties now, and if I think about a thing, a place, or a person long enough, I can recall memories from my childhood. It is all still there; I just need something to bring it to the surface.

The problem, Warren goes on to say, is that we don't realize how truly unique each of us is. DNA molecules can unite in an infinite number of ways. (The number is 10 to the 2,400,000,000th power.) That is the likelihood that you could ever find someone else just like you. You are fearfully and wonderfully made. You are unique. So be yourself.

Years ago, a Nike commercial featured the first draft pick of the NBA, Harold Miner. In the commercial he said some people asked him if he was going to be the next Magic Johnson, Larry Bird, or Michael Jordan. He told them, "I'm going to be the first Harold Miner." He ended up having less than a stellar career in the NBA, but it was still a cool commercial. And his point—to be yourself—was valid. The God who made us and knows us best did not make a mistake in gracing us with our unique mixture of talents and abilities.

There is a Hasidic tale of the Rabbi Zusya. When he was an old man, Zusya said, "In the coming world, they will not ask me: 'Why were you not Moses?' They will ask me: 'Why were you not Zusya?'" That is God's question to each of us as well. We are not expected to be who we are not—only who we are.

Therefore, give yourself to being whoever you are. I've heard that Erma Bombeck once said, "When I stand before God at the end of my life, I would hope that I would not have a single bit of talent left, and could say, 'I used everything you gave me.'" We need to be able to say the same. Remember that you are not a copy; you are an original. Be yourself.

People Can Move 

The second biblical truth you need to know about yourself is that you are not your past. No matter your past, no matter how you were raised or what failures may have marked you, you don't have to stay the way you are.

In *Silent for Sixty Years*, Ben Fainer tells how, when he was a nine-year-old child, the Nazis invaded Poland, separated him from his family, and placed him in a concentration camp. He managed to survive the Holocaust and told his story sixty years later. He wrote, "Mountains can't move, but people can."[6] What a marvelous truth. Mountains with all their splendor and grandeur are destined to stay mountains. Not so with you and me. We can move. We can become what we are gifted to be by the grace of God, even when life throws its worst at us.

You have no control over when and where you were born, who your parents were, your IQ, your genetic makeup, your color, your economic status, or your susceptibility to disease. But you are free to determine what happens to you.

Carl Sandburg once said, "There's an eagle in me that wants to soar, but there is also a hippopotamus in me that wants to wallow in the mud." We are all a bundle of contradictions and cross pulls. If you need a Scripture to back that up, try Romans 7:19, "For what I do is not the good I want to do; no the evil I do not want to do—this I keep on doing." However, don't forget that you decide where you go in life.

In his book *Craddock Stories*, seminary professor Fred Craddock told a great story about life's choices. One morning on vacation with his wife in Tennessee, they went out to breakfast hoping to enjoy a quiet family meal. While they were waiting for their food they noticed a distinguished, white haired man moving from table to table, visiting with the guests. Dr. Craddock said he leaned over and whispered to his wife, "I hope he doesn't come over here." But sure enough the man came over to the table.

> "Where are you folks from?" he asked in a friendly voice.

"Oklahoma" they answered.

"Great to have you here in Tennessee" the man said. "What do you do for a living?"

"I teach at a seminary," Dr. Craddock replied.

"Oh, so you teach preachers how to preach, do you? Well, I've got a really great story for you."

And with that, the gentleman pulled up a chair and sat down at the table with the couple. Dr. Craddock said he groaned and thought to himself, "Great . . . just what I need."

The man started, "See that mountain over there?" pointing at the restaurant window. "Not far from the base of that mountain was a boy born to an unwed mother. He had a hard time growing up because every place he went, he was always asked the same question, 'Hey boy, who's your daddy?' Whether he was at school, at the grocery store, or drug store, people would always ask the same question, 'Who's your daddy?'

"He would hide at recess and lunchtime from the other students. He would avoid going into stores because that question hurt him so bad. When he was about twelve years old, a new preacher came to his church. He would always go in late and slip out early to avoid hearing the question, 'Who's your daddy?' But one day the new preacher said the benediction so fast he got caught and had to walk out with the crowd.

"Just about the time he got to the back door, the new preacher, not knowing anything about him, put his hand on his shoulder and asked him, 'Son, who's your daddy?' The whole church got deathly quiet. He could feel every eye in the church looking at him. Now everyone would finally know the answer to the question, 'Who's your daddy?' This new preacher, though, sensed the situation around him and using discernment that only the Holy Spirit could give, said the following to that scared little boy.

"'Wait a minute! I know who you are. I see the family resemblance now. You are a child of God.' With that he patted the boy on his backside and said, 'Boy, you've got a great inheritance. Go and claim it.'

"With that, the boy smiled for the first time in a long time and walked out the door a changed person. He was never the same again.

"Whenever anybody asked him, 'Who's your daddy?' he'd just tell them, 'I'm a child of God.'"

The distinguished gentleman got up from the table and said, "Isn't that a great story?"

The professor responded that it really was a great story!

As the man turned to leave he said, "You know, if that new preacher hadn't told me that I was one of God's children, I never would have amounted to anything." And he walked away.

Dr. Craddock and his wife were stunned. He called the waitress over and asked her, "Do you know who that man was who just left that was sitting at our table?"

> The waitress grinned and said, "Of course, everyone here knows him. That's Ben Hooper. He's the former governor of Tennessee!"[7]

Someone in your life needs to remind you that you're one of God's children. You're not your past. By his grace, you can become something more. *Have a Little Faith* is the true story of author Mitch Albom, whose friend reminds him in the midst of a failure that Jesus is "the greatest recycler I know."[8] He can make something worthwhile from our failures and our mistakes. So remember that you are not your past.

Made for Eternity 

If you really want to know who you are, you must also realize that you are not made for time but for eternity. The Scriptures say, "He has made everything beautiful in its time. He has also set eternity in the hearts of men . . ." (Ecclesiastes 3:11). I believe as C.S. Lewis once said, "If I find in myself desires that nothing in this world can satisfy, the only logical explanation is that I was made for another world."[9]

A *Psalm of Life* by Henry Wadsworth Longfellow (1807-1882) expresses this truth so well:

> Tell me not in mournful numbers,
> Life is but an empty dream!
> For the soul is dead that slumbers,
> And things are not what they seem.

Life is real! Life is earnest!
And the grave is not the goal;
Dust thou art, to dust returneth,
Was not spoken of the soul.

He made us for eternity because he loves us and wants us to be with him forever. Buckner Fanning, former pastor of Trinity Baptist Church in San Antonio, Texas, gave me a new understanding of God's love expressed in Isaiah 49:16, "I have engraved you on the palms of my hands." He pointed out that George Adam Smith, the great Hebrew scholar, says the word "engraved" could best be translated as "tattooed." God has tattooed each of us on the palms of his hands.

To further illustrate this point, Buckner shared the following story in his book *God Drives a Pickup Truck*. He writes:

> On a trip to Honolulu, I noticed a tattoo shop near our hotel. Wanting to do some serious biblical research and, at the same time, desiring that my motives be conceived as pure, I asked my wife Martha to go with me. Her initial shock indicated that she consider a tattoo parlor on the level of a house of ill repute.
>
> After I picked Martha off the floor, I used my best Baptist oratory to convince her that tattoo parlors were legal and safe—relatively safe. Finally, she reluctantly agreed to accompany me, probably because she wanted evidence to complete

commitment papers on me. Or perhaps she wanted to be able to defend me if a San Antonio television station produced a flash TV report: "Baptist Preacher Buckner Fanning Visits Honolulu Tattoo Parlor."

When we entered the tattoo parlor, we met the manager, a woman whose body was covered with tattoos. At least everything we could see was tattooed. The manager looked at me as if I were an escapee from an asylum when I told her who I was. Thankfully, Martha provided some credibility, and the manager's skepticism turned to enthusiastic support when I quoted Isaiah 49:16 as the reason for my curiosity about tattoos.

This bright, young Swede shared a number of books and reference works on tattoos. We learned all we wanted to know about tattoos. For example, tattooing is an ancient art form dating back thousands of years. Surgery may remove most of a tattoo, but the surgical scar will remain. A skin graft fails to completely eliminate evidence of a tattoo because skin pigmentation cannot be accurately duplicated. Tattoos are as permanent as our physical features.

Then I asked, "What is the most sensitive part of the body to be tattooed?"

I thought the most sensitive area might be the face or some private part of the body. I was wrong. The most sensitive part of the human body to be tattooed is the palm of the hand and the top of the foot. I was amazed!

Suddenly, I understood more about what God was saying. His word was fantastic. God tattoos our name upon the palms of his hands and there is no way he can forget us—no way he can erase us from his hands. We are forever one with him, and in him. A spiritual explosion erupted in my mind as the crucifixion of Jesus took on a new and deeper significance.

When Jesus was nailed to the cross they "tattooed" him with nails in his hands and his feet—the most sensitive parts of his body. The scars from those wounds would never be erased.

A few days after the crucifixion and resurrection, when the disciple Thomas, "Doubting Thomas," saw those scars in the hands of the resurrected Christ, he exclaimed, "My Lord and my God."

Thomas saw those scars as the ineradicable sign of God's enduring love for him—a love that lasts forever!

What Thomas came to know, we can know! If we, like Thomas need help in overcoming our doubting moments, we can recall the "tattoos of Jesus and know that each of us is engraved on the palms of God's hands."

Those recollections provide us comfort that will bring us through the darkest hours of life, for "His love endures forever."[10]

Be assured, therefore, that God has a tender affection for you and for me. We were never intended for time alone but for eternity with him. Ponder that sailor's question to Kirk Douglas if you haven't already, "Hey! Do you know who you are?" If you do, you'll discover where you came from, what you've come through, and what you've come to. But remember also that you are an original, not a copy; you are not your past; and you were not made just for time but for eternity.

NOTES

1. http://articles.orlandosentinel.com/1988-09-09/life-style/0060450254_1_ragman-kirk-douglas-danielovitch. Accessed 1/4/16.
2. Kirk Douglas, *The Ragman's Son* (New York, NY: Simon & Schuster, 1982).
3. Kevin Belmonte, *A Journey Through the Life of William Wilberforce* (Green Forest, AR: New Leaf Press, 2006), 48–49.
4. Rick Warren, *The Purpose Driven Life* (Grand Rapids, MI: Zondervan Publishing House, 2002), 235.
5. Ibid.
6. Ben Fraimer, *Silent for Sixty Years: Ben Fraimer, Holocaust Survivor*, (Seattle, WA: CreateSpace Independent Publishing Platform, 2012).
7. Fred Craddock, *Craddock Stories* (Atlanta, GA: Chalice Press, 2001), 156–157.
8. Mitch Albom, *Have a Little Faith* (New York, NY: Hachette Press, 2011), 136.
9. http://www.lewissociety.org/quotes.php. Accessed 1/16/16.
10. Buckner Fanning, *God Drives a Pickup Truck* (Indianapolis, IN: LifeWorks Publishing, 1999), 100–101.

Over time, we see the Church–warts and all–and we can get disillusioned. Then we realize the Church is a divine institution with human flaws. We never outgrow our need for the fellowship and the strength it provides, so don't neglect it.

10

Stay in Church

Malachi 1:13; Hebrews 10:24–25

A man came home on a Friday night after a hard week's work and told his wife, "Sweetheart, let's go somewhere for the weekend where we're not known or recognized."

His wife responded, "How about going to church?"

In the Scriptures, it's clear that church attendance is important in the Christian life. Jesus set the example by attending the synagogue "as was his custom" on the Sabbath day. The Bible encourages us not to neglect regular worship and the inspiration and mutual encouragement it provides. Unfortunately, some were already doing that in the early days of the Christian Church (Hebrews 10:25). And many more are still doing so today.

People drop out of church for many reasons. It's usually a reflection of their own spiritual temperature more than the church itself. But there is one thing worse than not attending church at all—to go without investing your heart in it. Unfortunately, many are absent during the time they take up the most space.

In the days of Malachi the prophet, religion had reached a low ebb. The people continued attending worship services, but worship had ceased to be vital and meaningful. The prophet described them as attending church but saying in their hearts, "What a burden it is" (Malachi 1:13). This accusation, in a time when Israel's spiritual life was in a steep decline, describes a faith that had degenerated into a cold, formal, external type of religion. The people had become cynical and godless. Even the priests were unholy, unspiritual, and skeptical.

So backslidden were the people that they brought their blind, crippled, and diseased animals as sacrifices to God. The corrupt priests not only accepted them but also encouraged the practice. Moreover, since their worship never translated itself into daily living, they dishonored their marriage vows and robbed God of his tithes and offerings. They offered as a sacrifice what they would not dare to offer to the governor.

They would not give themselves wholeheartedly to the Lord, yet they were not prepared to abandon him altogether.

They kept up regular attendance even as they silently sighed how worship had become a dull, monotonous routine instead of a meaningful experience.

Today, if all the people who shared these feelings should say "Amen" at once, it would be a shout heard around the world. They, too, feel a weariness in going to church. Like Israel, they are neither prepared to abandon God completely, nor are they ready to follow him wholeheartedly. So they settle down to meaningless church attendance. They listlessly pick up a hymnal and mumble through the words. They drop a token in the collection plates as they go by, constantly glancing at their watch and wondering, "When will this end so we can get out of here and do something important?"

If you are going to church more and enjoying it less, maybe you need to look at your own heart and consider the totality of worship. For the truth is, meaningless worship not only wearies the people, it also wearies the Lord (Mal. 2:17). In Malachi's time, as it is today, three things can cause worship to weary both the people and the Lord:

- We grow weary of church when leaders are not respected.
- We grow weary of church when God is not reverenced.
- We grow weary of church when our faith in not relevant.

Whenever we experience those three truths, something needs to change because we need to stay in church.

You Go First 

First, going to church can be wearying when the leaders are not honorable. As I pointed out, the priests of Malachi's day did not honor God's name and allowed the people to get by with second-class sacrifices. When God's appointed leaders are not who they ought to be, the Church is not what it ought to be.

Repeatedly in Scripture the Lord warns against professional prophets who, instead of being watchmen over the people, were guilty of seeking unjust gains for themselves (Isaiah 56:11). For example, Jeremiah accuses the priests of leading the people away from the Lord instead of closer to him (Jeremiah 50:6). Ezekiel accuses them of: being fat and lazy, feeding themselves rather than feeding the flock, and failing to minister to the needs of the people (Ezekiel 34:1–10). Even the Apostle Paul warns of wolves in sheep's clothing (Acts 20:29).

Incompetent leadership has plagued the Church for much of the time since then. Kevin Belmonte wrote about church leaders in 17th century England:

> The Church which some might have expected to serve as a beacon of moral authority, was itself plagued by immorality and apathy, and a mere nominal belief in the Christian creeds was commonplace. It was said that "the spirit of religions slumbered."

> Members of the clergy were absent from their churches, often more concerned with hunting and playing cards. This led to the neglect of the spiritual and physical needs of the congregation.
>
> Anna Moore, the popular playwright, who also became a Christian largely through the influence of hymn writer and pastor John Newton, described the church conditions she encountered in rural England about this time. In Axbridge, Somerset, she learned that a preacher named Gould was "drunk about six times a week, kept a mistress in his house, and very frequently was prevented from preaching by two black eyes he got by fighting."[1]

Dishonorable leadership still plagues the Church today. Pedophile priests, fake faith healers, charlatan TV evangelists, preachers of health and wealth, and name-it-and-claim-it theology are still around in abundance. I remember when television personality Bill O'Reilly once interviewed an atheist who was a proponent of Darwin's theory of evolution. Immediately afterwards, O'Reilly interviewed comedian-actor Dennis Miller and asked if he believed in God.

Miller said, "I believe that somebody made Darwin. Yes, I bend my knee to God and pray."

When O'Reilly asked if he was Catholic, Miller said yes and added, "But the last time I went to confession I said to the priest, 'You go first.'"

You go first. That's a fair proposition. The implication was, of course, that the priest needed to get his life right with God first and then hear the confession of others. O'Reilly then countered, "But you can't doubt the theology because of the priest."

Dennis responded, "I don't doubt the script (i.e., the Bible), but I do question the current cast." I once knew a lady who said, "I'm going to church even if the devil is in the pulpit." Sometimes he is, but stay in church anyway. It will help you no matter what.

Offer it to the Governor

Second, worship is wearying when God is not reverenced. By offering the animals nobody wanted, the people were simply a reflection of their leaders. They most always are. Malachi challenged people to offer crippled animals to the governor and see if he would accept them. Then he reminded them that God is a great King, worthy of their highest and best. When we bring our second best to God and sacrifice our leftovers, worship loses its luster. Remember, it not only wearies us; it also wearies God.

You may be thinking, "I didn't know we were still supposed to make sacrifices to God." That is true of animal sacrifices. Jesus is the "Lamb of God" who takes away the sins of the world. He offered his life "once and for all" as a sacrifice for our sin, not on the altar of the temple, but on the cross of Calvary. So effective was the sacrifice of Jesus that never again would humanity have to offer up the blood of bulls and goats as an atonement for their sins (Heb. 9:23–28).

But while the Scriptures make it clear that animal sacrifice has passed away, they nowhere suggest that God has abolished the principle of sacrifice in true worship. God has not abdicated the principle of sacrifice; he has only changed the form. God is no longer interested in a dead animal. What he wants is a living person. In fact, the Bible gives us at least four sacrifices that we should offer to the Lord.

First, we should offer ourselves. The Apostle Paul encourages us to present our bodies, our whole selves, as a sacrifice unto God. This involves our ears, eyes, hands, lips, feet—our entire being (Romans 12:1–2).

In World War II, the courtyard of a little church in France held a statue of Christ with his arms outstretched over the village below. One day a bomb exploded too near the church, and the statue was destroyed. The people could not bear the thought of their village without the statue of Jesus watching over it, so they patiently and diligently gathered the fragments and pieced them together to remake it.

The final result was covered with scars and scratches, but they decided it enhanced the statue rather than detracted from it. However, they could not find the hands of Christ. A statue with nicks was fine, but a statue with no hands just would not do. Then someone came up with the idea of placing a placard at the base of the statue that read: "I have no hands but yours." That's what Paul has in mind when he appeals to us to present a sacrifice of our bodies to Christ.

Second, we are to offer our praise, the fruit of our lips (Heb. 13:15). Music is the language of the soul. Whatever we feel deeply about, we soon sing about—love, home, country, mother, and, of course, God. Music also inspires and encourages others around us. Paul writes that we are to speak "to one another with psalms, hymns, and spiritual songs. Sing and make music in your heart to the Lord" (Ephesians 5:19). And again, "Let the message of Christ dwell in you richly as you teach and admonish one another with all wisdom, and as you sing psalms, hymns, and spiritual songs with gratitude in your hearts to God" (Colossians 3:16).

Praise has always been a part of true worship. I once saw an advertisement in the newspaper that read, "The Ebenezer Baptist Church will have its regular worship service on the first Sunday of the month. Three books of worship will be used, the hymnbook, the Holy Book, and the pocketbook. Come and bring all three." It should be so today. So when we offer up the sacrifice of praise, let us do it with our whole hearts. Toscanini, the great conductor, would quite often say to his orchestra as they rehearsed, "Don't play with your instruments. Play with your hearts." Likewise, when we sing in church, let us sing heartily as unto the Lord.

Third, we should offer our service (Heb. 13:16). R.C. Buckner, who founded Buckner's Benevolences years ago, said as he was dying, "Please do not fold my hands across my breast. Leave them open, ready for work. I had such joy and profit here. I trust the Master will have something for me to do hereafter. Leave my hands open for more service."

I don't know what he will have for us to do in the hereafter, but I do know there is plenty for us to do in the here and now. Doing it is a sacrifice we offer to God.

Finally, we should offer our gifts to God (Heb. 13:16). When the Apostle Paul was in prison in Rome, the church in Philippi sent a love offering to help him in his ministry. He invested that gift with the sacredness of an Old Testament sacrifice when he called it "a fragrant offering, an acceptable sacrifice, pleasing to God" (Philippians 4:18). Their gift was like a burnt offering, and the pleasant smell flowed up to the nostrils of God. Christina Rossetti's tiny poem from 1872 summarizes it best:

> What can I give Him, poor as I am?
> If I were a shepherd, I would bring a lamb;
> If I were a Wise Man, I would do my part;
> Yet what I can I give Him: give my heart.

For the Home as Well as the Church 

The third truth about worship is that it is wearying when our faith is not related to life. Our faith is not just for Sunday but for Monday through Saturday as well. It is not just for the church but also for the home and the workplace. God has committed himself to all of life. He concerns himself not only with man's religious life but also with his whole life. Malachi focuses on two areas in particular where the people do not relate what they are taught to the way they live—their marriage and their money.

First, he says that the Lord was a witness when they took their marriage vows. Instead of keeping their promise to God and to one another, they were getting divorced. Then the Lord says unequivocally, "I hate divorce" (Mal. 2:16). He did then, and he still does now.

There can be no doubt that God's idea for marriage is one man and one woman living together for life. But while God hates divorce, he loves the divorcée. This does not mean that he condones the behavior, but he still loves and accepts the people who have failed in their relationships.

Divorce is often the lesser of two evils. Choices in life are not always between good and evil, right and wrong, black and white. Sometimes the choices are between bad and worse. While divorce is wrong, so is alcoholism, child abuse, homosexuality, perversion, and spousal abuse. It is better to divorce in such instances and live in peace. Marriage is not to be held together at all cost.

The Christian faith calls for unconditional love and forgiveness for anyone who comes to God with an attitude of repentance, but we cannot lower the standard to accommodate the culture. When we do, worship becomes meaningless or, even worse, wearisome. God makes it clear, "I the LORD do not change" (Mal. 3:6).

Second, Malachi reproves the people for not tithing. His accusation is severe, "Will a man rob God? Yet you rob me. But you ask, 'How do we rob you?' In tithes and offerings'" (Mal. 3:8). Failure to tithe is stealing from God and from his work through the Church. Then comes the challenge to bring our tithes into his house, and he will open the windows of heaven and pour out a blessing on us that there is not room enough to receive. When we fail to give as we ought to do, we not only rob God of what is rightfully his, and the Church of its needed resources to carry on his work, but we also rob ourselves of God's blessings.

If we're right in our marriage and with our money, we're likely to be right in most other areas of life. One thing is sure: worship will never be joyous unless we practice in our daily lives what we profess in church. At the end of life, we will be evaluated and rewarded based on how we handled what God entrusted to us.

Others may violate their sacred vows to God, but don't you do it. Stay in church, and the blessings will come. As William Wilberforce once said, "Let reform begin and let it begin with me." That's where real reform begins—both in society and in the Church.

The challenge then, is that we are always to give God our highest and our best. We should expect our leaders to practice what they preach. And we must translate what we hear on Sunday into our daily lives the rest of the week. If we'll do that, worship will be wonderful instead of wearisome, and we'll stay in church.

NOTES

1. Kevin Belmonte, *A Journey Through the Life of William Wilberforce* (Green Forest, AR: New Leaf Press, 2006), 68.

With age, everything goes—
including our hearing.
Even if you have to wear a
hearing aid, don't forget to
listen for the trumpet.
It will be music to your ears.

11

Listen for the Trumpet

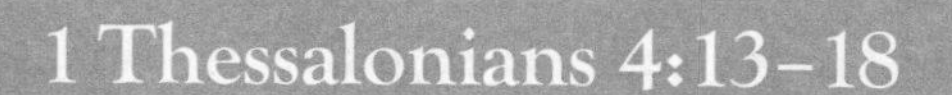

The world has not seen the last of Jesus Christ. We have God's word on that—in prophecy, his promise, and New Testament preaching. The Scriptures proclaim that the Savior must suffer and die for the sins of the world. Isaiah wrote,

> But he was pierced for our transgressions, he was crushed for our iniquities; the punishment

> that brought us peace was upon him, and by his wounds we are healed. We all, like sheep, have gone astray, each of us has turned to his own way; and the LORD has laid on him the iniquity of us all (Isaiah 53:5–6).

David declared that he would be raised from the dead when he wrote, ". . . you will not abandon me to the grave, nor will you let your Holy One see decay" (Psalm 16:10). To this, the Apostle Paul adds,

> We tell you the good news: What God promised our fathers he has fulfilled for us, their children, by raising up Jesus. As it is written in the second Psalm, "You are my Son; today I have become your Father." The fact that God raised him from the dead, never to decay, is stated in these words: "I will give you the holy and sure blessings promised to David." So it is stated elsewhere: "You will not let your Holy One see decay" (Acts 13:32–35).

Jesus himself promised he would return when he said, "And if I go and prepare a place for you, I will come back and take you to be with me that you also may be where I am" (John 14:3). The apostles proclaim this truth throughout Scripture, including 1 Thessalonians 4:13–18. They believed that Jesus would come again and take his people home to heaven to be with him. This was their ultimate hope.

They often taught that "time is short" (1 Corinthians 7:29), "the Lord's coming is near" (James 5:8), and "the end of all things is near" (1 Peter 4:7). Paul's teaching in 1 Corinthians 7 on celibacy was based on his belief that Christ would soon return. It was his opinion that since time was short, it would be better for believers to be single, as he was, so they could better serve Christ without family distractions.

Early Christians were expecting Jesus to return very soon, and they fully expected to be alive when he came back. But his delay brought a special problem to these believers. Some had died, and their family and friends were not sure if they would share in that great event. They were questioning what part these dead believers would play in the divine drama at the end of time. Paul wrote to clear up their misunderstandings, "Brothers, we do not want you to be ignorant about those who fall asleep, or to grieve like the rest of men, who have no hope" (1 Thessalonians 4:13).

In the face of death, the pagan world stood in despair, meeting it with grim resignation and bleak hopelessness. Again and again their philosophers wrote that those who are alive have hope, but those who died were hopeless. At best, they saw them as asleep in one perpetual night. There was no expectation of life beyond the grave, no belief in a resurrection, no reunion with their loved ones.

The Apostle Paul contrasted that with Christian hope. He said,

> We believe that Jesus died and rose again, and so we believe that God will bring with Jesus those who have fallen asleep in him. According to the

> Lord's own word, we tell you that we who are still alive, who are left till the coming of the Lord, will certainly not precede those who have fallen asleep. For the Lord himself will come down from heaven, with a loud command, with the voice of the archangel and with the trumpet call of God, and the dead in Christ will rise first. After that, we who are still alive and are left will be caught up together with them in the clouds to meet the Lord in the air. And so we will be with the Lord forever. Therefore encourage each other with these words (1 Thess. 4:14–18).

Paul wrote in a straightforward manner—Jesus will come again, and when he does the dead will be raised, the living will be transformed, and we will all be with the Lord and with one another forever. In the clearest possible statement, this is our Christian hope. It is resurrection, rapture, and reunion at his coming.

The Apostle Paul described this as a single event. There is no mention of two comings, just one. Some people, however, are not satisfied with so simple an explanation. So, they have taken a few passages from the Old Testament and a few passages from the New Testament (some they've interpreted literally and some symbolically) to piece together elaborate theories that explain in detail how all these events will unfold. However, the result is like a picture of a jigsaw puzzle with some of the pieces missing. Then they color the empty spaces in to fit their own theory.

Nowhere does God give us a more complete picture in one place than what is recorded here. I have to believe that if he wanted us to know all the details regarding the timing and sequence of future events, he would have made it less complicated. These man-made theories satisfy people's curiosity and provide exciting sermon topics, but they do little else.

I have preached and pastored for sixty years. I have read all the theories of men, but they have done little to improve on this simple statement. I steer clear of man's theories and ideas, trying my best to stick with the simple teachings of the Scriptures. Not subscribing to these theories has not lessened my evangelistic fervor. It has always been a priority with me. Nor has it limited my ability to grow people to be like Christ or to build his Church.

Why not be content with what is said here? Christ will return, and when he does, the resurrection will occur, God's people will be raptured out of the earth, and they will be together with him forever. What else really matters?

I realize that it does not answer all of our questions. For example, people want to know when Jesus will come again. However, Jesus said he didn't know. He explained, "But about that day or hour no one knows, not even the angels in heaven, nor the Son, but only the Father" (Matthew 24:36). If he didn't know, I certainly don't. It is enough to know that I should be ready when it happens.

People also wonder what kind of body we will have in the resurrection. Paul spoke extensively to that in 1 Corinthians 15:35–50. He summarized, "And just as we have borne the likeness of the earthly man, so shall we bear the likeness of the man from heaven" (1 Cor. 15:49). And then again he adds,

> But our citizenship is in heaven. And we eagerly await a Savior from there, the Lord Jesus Christ, who, by the power that enables him to bring everything under his control, will transform our lowly bodies so that they will be like his glorious body (Philippians 3:20–21).

What about the unsaved? No mention is made of them in this passage. We must go to passages like Revelation 22:11–15 to answer that question. But for now, and for us, this is our hope. We need only to be ready; the details are up to him.

Consider the following truths about the Christian's hope in the face of death:

- Our hope is the resurrection of the dead.
- Our hope is the rapture of believers.
- Our hope is the reunion of God's people with him and with one another in heaven.

In the meantime, we need to be busy serving Christ, ready to meet him, and listening for the trumpet to sound. In the following pages, let's explore each dimension of this eternal hope.

Cemetery Traffic

The resurrection of the dead is the first essential reason for our hope. The opening event that will occur when the trumpet sounds and Christ returns is that "the dead in Christ will rise" (1 Thess. 4:16). The word "resurrection" literally means "to stand again." Those who are dead will stand up alive again after they have died. Death does not have the last word. The grave is not the victor, God is! Our hope one day is that graves at the cemetery will open, and the dead in Christ will stand up alive again. Today the cemetery is the deadest place in town. One day it will be the liveliest place where all the action is!

You may ask, "How can we be sure there will be a resurrection since there has never been one before?" Our assurance is based solely on the resurrection of Jesus; not human speculation, human sentiment, or even logic. It rests in him alone (1 Thess. 4:14).

The Scriptures speak of Jesus as "the first fruits of those who have fallen asleep" (1 Cor. 15:20). "First fruits" is an agricultural term that describes the first heads of grain that ripen in the field in late spring and early summer. They were sacred to the Jews because they marked the beginning of the harvest and the pledge of more to come. If there were no first fruits, then there would be no harvest later on. If there were no beginning, there would be no reason to expect an end. They were so important that the Jews offered them as a sacrifice to God.

To say that Jesus is the first fruits of the resurrection is to say that he is the beginning of that event. He is God's pledge to us that there will be a general resurrection at the end of time. If anyone should ask you when the resurrection is going to take place, you should respond, "It already started when Jesus was raised from the dead." If anyone should ask you how you are sure there will be a resurrection, simply say, "Because Jesus has already been raised from the dead."

And if that's not enough, tell them he said so, for Jesus explained,

> Do not be amazed at this, for a time is coming when all who are in their graves will hear his voice and come out—those who have done good will rise to live, and those who have done evil will rise to be condemned (John 5:28–29).

And again at the graveside of Lazarus, he proclaimed, "I am the resurrection and the life. He who believes in me will live, even though he dies" (John 11:25).

This is the blessed hope of every believer. When Jesus returns to the earth, the graves in the cemetery will be open and the dead will stand up again just as he stood up in the tomb. We shall live again. Still, there are many questions left unanswered. For example, what about those who have been cremated? If the sea can give up the dead in it to face God in the judgment (Rev. 20:13), surely the crematorium can give up the dead that are in it.

Will there be animals in heaven? A lady asked me that question just this week. When Isaiah spoke of the coming kingdom, he wrote, "The wolf will live with the lamb, the leopard will lie down with the goat, the calf and the lion and the yearling together; and a little child will lead them" (Isa. 11:6). This verse suggests that there will be animals in heaven. In fact, Isaiah says that in the Messiah's reign there will be harmony in the whole of creation, including the animals.

Then of course the age-old question, "What will happen between death and the resurrection?" The Scriptures say that when Jesus comes again he will bring with him those who have "fallen asleep in him" (1 Thess. 4:14). They are already with him. Their body is in the grave, but their spirit is with the Lord. Maybe an epitaph found on a grave in Nantucket, Massachusetts, explains it best:

> Under the sod and under the trees
>   Lies the body of John Pease.
> He's not here, only the pod
>   Pease shelled out and went to God.

While in prison in Philippi awaiting trial and possible execution, the Apostle Paul speaks of standing at the crossroads of life and death and having a hard time deciding which of the two he preferred. His desire was to depart this life and be with Christ. His sense of duty, however, was to remain and help the churches. In one instance, he wanted to see Christ; in the other, he wanted to serve Christ (Phil. 1:23–25). Death meant he would be with Christ. There is nothing of the idea of his going to sleep in the grave. Again he spoke of death as being "away from the body and at home with the Lord" (2 Corinthians 5:8). There is no hint that we will go to the grave and sleep there until eternity. To leave this body (and that's what death is) is to be "at home with the Lord."

This great event will happen when the trumpet sounds and the Lord returns. Are you listening for the trumpet?

Suddenly They're Gone 

Our hope is also founded upon the rapture of the believers. The second event that will happen when Christ returns concerns the living saints who will "be caught up together with them in the clouds . . ." (1 Thess. 4:17). The words "caught up" come from the Latin word that means "rapture." If we are fortunate enough to be alive when Jesus comes again, our bodies will be transformed without having to die. We will be changed in an instant and raptured into heaven.

Jesus spoke of this event when he said, "Two men will be in the field; one will be taken and the other left. Two women will be grinding with a hand mill; one will be taken and the other left" (Matt. 24:40–41). One will be taken to the Lord and life. The other will be taken to judgment and death.

Only two people in Scripture were taken to heaven without having to experience the death process. The first was Enoch. The Scriptures say of him, "Enoch walked with God; then he was no more, for God took him away"

(Gen. 5:24; Hebrews 11:5). The word "walked" literally means "walked about" (i.e., he lived in fellowship with God). Instead of letting him die, God just took him home to be with him.

Elijah was the second person to go to heaven without experiencing death (2 Kings 2:11). He was caught up into heaven in a whirlwind. Both went to heaven directly without dying, as will all believers who are alive at his coming.

While we will not have to die, we will have to be transformed, for flesh and blood cannot inherit the kingdom of heaven (1 Cor. 15:50). We will be given a new body that is not subject to the ravages of death, nor the decay of time. It will be like the resurrection body of Jesus (1 Cor. 15:49). Paul says Jesus will "transform our lowly bodies so that they will be like his glorious body" (Phil. 3:21).

What will heaven be like? Pastor R.G. Lee once said, "Heaven is the most beautiful place the mind of God could conceive and the hand of God could create." The Apostle John saw heaven as a bride adorned for her husband. A young lady is never more beautiful than she is on her wedding day. More preparation has gone into her appearance that day than on any day prior. Heaven reminds John of that kind of unspeakable beauty. Then he adds that there will be no blind eyes in heaven. No twisted limbs up there. No ambulances screaming down golden streets. No funeral wreaths hanging on mansion doors. Old things will have passed away and all things will become new.

Change is coming—change in us and change in the world. Are you listening for the trumpet?

Gathered to Our People 

The final reason for Christian hope is that when the trumpet sounds and Jesus comes again, there will be a glad reunion in the sky. The resurrected dead and the raptured living will be "caught up together with them" in the clouds. "And so we will be with the Lord forever" (1 Thess. 4:17).

Note those two phrases side-by-side: "with them" and "with the Lord." Both speak of the glad reunion that we'll experience in heaven. This is no new idea for the people of God. The Scriptures say that Abraham died and was "gathered to his people;" Isaac died and was "gathered to his people;" Jacob died and was "gathered to his people." What can that phrase mean? It cannot mean that they were taken back to the old family cemetery to be buried next to their family members. After all, Abraham's people were buried in distant Ur of the Chaldeans.

Years later, the Lord said of Moses that he would die and be "gathered to your people" (Deuteronomy 32:50). Then when Moses died, the Lord buried him in an unmarked grave on a windswept mountain overlooking the Promised Land. There was no one in attendance but God and the angels. There was no marker. No flowers. No mourners. Moses being "gathered" to his people could not possibly mean being buried next to his loved ones. Miriam's body was buried in the desert. Aaron was buried on Mount Hor, and his mother was buried in the sands of Egypt. It must mean that he was gathered to his people in glory where they had gone on before.

Consider also the story of King David. He had a child who was sick unto death. For many days, the child held on to the slender thread of life. These were days of agony and anxiety for David. He sat in constant vigil over his son and went without food and sleep. He prayed and fasted with the hope that the child might live. Nothing—not the demands of his high office, nor the appeals of his servants, nor the needs of his own life—could take him away from his vigil.

When the boy finally died, David's servants were greatly distressed. They did not know how to break the news to him and even feared that in his despair he might take his own life. As they were trying to decide how to tell him, he saw them whispering. He asked, "Is the child dead?" They answered, "Yes."

Then to their amazement, David rose, washed himself, changed his clothes, and went immediately to the house of God and worshipped. Then he returned to the palace and asked for a meal. His servants were bewildered. They could not understand why he had fasted and prayed while the child was alive, but now the child was dead and he was resuming the normal activities of his life. His servants asked for an explanation.

David's answer is worth remembering:

> While the child was still alive, I fasted and wept. I thought, 'Who knows? The Lord may be gracious to me and let the child live.' But now that he is dead, why should I fast? Can I bring him back again? I will go to him, but he will not return to me (2 Samuel 12:22–23).

This is the same David who wrote in Psalm 23, "Even though I walk through the valley of the shadow of death, I will fear no evil, for you are with me . . . and I will dwell in the house of the Lord forever." His hope? "I shall go to him."

By the way, it would be a sad ending to the great life of Moses if we left him buried all alone on the mountainside. But walk with me up another mountain 800 years later. It is the Mount of Transfiguration. Jesus has taken his disciples Peter, James, and John to a high mountain where they receive a visual demonstration and hear an audible voice declaring him to be the Son of God. Going alone to pray, Jesus takes on the glow of heaven and reveals his divinity. Then a voice from heaven announces, "This is my Son, whom I love; with him I am well pleased" (Matt. 17:5).

Suddenly Moses and Elijah appear with Jesus, their presence also attesting to the fact that Jesus is the Son of God. Will we know each other in heaven? Surely we will, since apparently the disciples immediately recognized Moses and Elijah without benefit of introductions or nametags. It suggests to me that in heaven we will not only know each other, but also those whom we have never met. Paul says, "Now we see but a poor reflection as in a mirror; then we shall see face to face" (1 Cor. 13:12). Do we know each other here? Yes. Surely we will be smarter there than we are here.

William Barclay shares a story in his commentary of the New Testament about Queen Mary of Orange whose chaplain wished to read to her on her deathbed. She answered him, "I have not left this matter 'til this hour." We must not either. The time to decide is now. I remind you that Jesus will come as "a thief in the night." As it was in the days of Noah, there will be times of carousing and unpreparedness—so we must be ready when the trumpet sounds.

The question is, "Are you listening?"

The assurance that we are going to heaven is important at any age. But the less time we have left, the more we need to be sure of our destination for eternity.

12

Be Sure You're Going to Heaven

1 John 5:13

What does it mean to "know that you know?" Donald Rumsfeld, as Secretary of Defense, coined the phrase, "known knowns" to describe known facts in a military context. There are also some known knowns in the Christian life. For example, we *know* that God is at work for good in the lives of his children to make us more like Jesus Christ. The Scriptures say, "And we *know* that in all things God works for the good of those who love him, who have been called according to his purpose . . . to become conformed to the likeness of his Son . . ." (Romans 8:28–29).

In addition, the Bible says we can *know* that when our earthly body wears out, the Lord will give us a new and eternal body in heaven not made with hands. "Now we know that if the earthly tent we live in is destroyed, we have a building from God, an eternal house in heaven, not built by human hands" (2 Corinthians 5:1). Finally, we can also *know* that believers have everlasting life. Jesus said, "I tell you the truth, whoever hears my word and believes in him who sent me has eternal life and will not be condemned; he has crossed over from death to life" (John 5:24). Do not miss the progression of this verse from "hearing, to believing, to having." That's the pathway of assurance.

Can a person know he is going to heaven and be sure he has eternal life? Yes! The Apostle John writes, "I write these things to you who believe in the name of the Son of God so that you may *know* that you have eternal life" (1 John 5:13). How can we know we are going to heaven? How can we be sure we have eternal life? There are three answers:

- Because God's word says so.
- Because of the facts, our faith, and the fruit of the Spirit.
- Because of God's grace and his grip.

Arrogant or Presumptuous?

First, we can be sure of our salvation because God says so in 1 John 5:13. The entire book of 1 John deals with the subject of assurance, but this is the clearest statement in the book. Almost every word in that one verse is a key term to our understanding of assurance. So let's unpack the verse word-by-word.

John says he wants us to *know* we are saved. The word "know" means to have absolute and settled knowledge. Is it presumptuous to say that you know you are going to heaven? No, it is not arrogance to believe God. Nor is it presumptuous to take him at his word. It is humble knowledge of our present acceptance by God. We base this confidence on the finished work of Christ. It is not self-confidence, for the Scriptures say he saved us "not because of righteous things we had done, but because of his mercy" (Titus 3:5). We can "know that we know" and be assured of our assurance of salvation.

Standing on the Promises

Next, John says he has "written" certain things so we will know the truth. How then can you have assurance? It is easy. Find out what God wants you to do in order to be saved or forgiven by reading what he clearly says in the Bible. Then believe God and do it. Is he reliable? Is he truthful? Will he do what he says he will do? God cannot lie, and he keeps his word. Our assurance, therefore, is not based upon what we are or what we do, but rather upon God's reliable character.

Likewise, the Apostle Peter underscores the trustworthiness of God's word when he writes,

> We did not follow cleverly invented stories when we told you about the power and coming of our Lord Jesus Christ, but we were eyewitnesses of his majesty. For he received honor and glory from God the Father when the voice came to him from the Majestic Glory, saying, 'This is my Son, whom I love; with him I am well pleased.' We ourselves heard this voice that came from heaven when we were with him on the sacred mountain. And we have the word of the prophets made more certain, and you will do well to pay attention to it, as to a light shining in a dark place, until the day dawns and the morning star rises in your hearts (2 Peter 1:16–19).

As we discussed in the previous chapter, they saw Jesus transformed and heard the voice of God from heaven. To that, Peter adds, ". . . and we have the word of the prophets made *more* certain . . ." More certain than an eyewitness? Yes. More than an audible voice? Yes. We have the word of God, and it is more accurate than our eyes and our ears.

Our salvation is founded on the word of God, not on feelings. Martin Luther expressed it beautifully in his poem:

Feelings come and feelings go,
And feelings are deceiving;
My warranty is the word of God –
Naught else is worth believing.

Though my heart should feel condemned
For want of some sweet token,
There is one greater than my heart
Whose word cannot be broken.

I'll trust in God's unchanging word
Till soul and body sever,
For, though all things shall pass away,
HIS WORD SHALL STAND FOREVER!

When W.B. Glass, a long-time missionary to China, was on his deathbed in the darkness of the night, he cried out again and again: "Cling to the promises! Cling to the promises!" That's the basis of our assurance.

What Does God Expect?

Next, pay attention to what John writes in 1 John 5:13, "I have written to you who *believe* in the name of the Son of God." This is another way that you "know that you know." You know you believe in the Lord Jesus Christ.

When the Philippian jailer cried out to Paul and Silas, asking what he had to do to be saved, they told him to believe on the Lord Jesus Christ (Acts 16:31–32). Jesus, speaking to Nicodemus said, "For God so loved the world that he gave his one and only Son, that whoever believes in him shall not perish but have eternal life" (John 3:16). And again he said, "I tell you the truth, he who believes has everlasting life" (John 6:47).

What does it mean to believe? It is not simply intellectual assent. The Scriptures say that the demons also believe and "shudder" (James 2:19). They believe, but they do not trust. To believe means to trust in, to rely on, and to adhere to Jesus for our salvation.

In the 19th century, the greatest tightrope walker in the world was a man named Charles Blondin. On June 30, 1859, he became the first man in history to walk on a tightrope across Niagara Falls. Over 25,000 people gathered to watch him walk 1,100 feet suspended on a tiny rope 160 feet above the raging waters. He worked without a net or safety harness of any kind. The slightest slip would prove fatal. When he safely reached the Canadian side, the crowd burst into a mighty roar.

In the days that followed, he would walk across the Falls many times. Years ago, I heard Billy Graham tell about the time that "The Great Blondin" (as he was called) pushed a wheelbarrow across the water. He then asked the cheering spectators if they thought he could push a man across sitting in a wheelbarrow. A roar of approval rose from the crowd. Spying a man cheering loudly, he asked, "Sir, do you think I could safely carry you across in this wheelbarrow?"

"Yes, of course," said the man.

"Get in," the Great Blondin replied with a confident smile.

The man refused.

It's one thing to believe a man can walk across by himself. It's another thing to believe he could safely carry *you* across. It's something else entirely to get into the wheelbarrow yourself. It's not enough to believe that Christ theoretically could save you. Until you "get in the wheelbarrow" and trust all to him, you are not saved.

But I have some good news for you. Jesus has carried many people safely across the great divide, and he has never lost anyone yet. You can trust him.

The Name above Every Name 

The next part of this verse that we need to unpack is where John writes that we must believe in the "name" of the Son of God. Belief requires an object. We can't believe just anything. Names represent the essence of a person. That's why the Scriptures say not to take God's name in vain. The very name of Jesus means, "Jehovah is salvation." When Jesus was born, an angel told Mary and Joseph to name him Jesus "because he will save his people from their sins" (Matthew 1:21). The Scriptures are clear: "Salvation is found in no one else, for there is no other name under heaven given to men by which we must be saved" (Acts 4:12).

In his sermon to Cornelius and his household, Peter said, "All the prophets testify about him that everyone who believes in him receives forgiveness of sins through his name" (Acts 10:43). As a result of cultural influences, some have legitimized the Muslim religion and think that using the name "Allah" (the Arabic word for God) is just another way of worshiping the same God. Not so. The God of the Bible is Jehovah. He introduced himself to Moses at the burning bush as, "I am who I am." He told him to tell the Egyptians that "I am" had sent him (Exodus 3:6, 14). That name means the eternal, self-existing one; the God who was and is and evermore shall be. He's the God of salvation, the God of truth, and the God of life. Allah is the product of the warped mind of Mohammed in 10 AD, and they are *not* the same. Salvation is in the name of Jesus alone (John 14:1–6).

Eternal Life

Finally, John explains in 1 John 5:13 that the point of it all is so that we may have eternal life. We will all live forever—some in heaven and some in hell. Jesus said,

> Do not be amazed at this, for a time is coming when all who are in their graves will hear his voice and come out—those who have done good will rise to live, and those who have done evil will rise to be condemned (John 5:28–29).

He adds,

> When the Son of Man comes in his glory, and all the angels with him, he will sit on his throne in heavenly glory. All the nations will be gathered before him, and he will separate the people one from another as a shepherd separates the sheep from the goats. Then they will go away to eternal punishment, but the righteous to eternal life (Matt. 25:31–32, 46).

Eternal life refers to a quality of life, not just a quantity. It means that when you trust Christ, your life has been changed. You are not anxious about tomorrow. You learn to forgive others as you have been forgiven. You do unto others as you would have them do unto you. You help the poor and the needy. You are not angry with your brother. You do not lust. You do not covet.

The Scriptures speak of the fruit of the Spirit as love, joy, peace, patience, kindness, goodness, faithfulness, gentleness, and self-control (Galatians 5:22–23). These qualities will eventually develop in someone who possesses eternal life. James reminds us that faith without works is dead. Works and fruit are the same. If a person claims to have faith, and he does not have the works of righteousness that are consistent with it, then it is a dead faith (James 2:14–17).

So you can test yourself. In fact, Scripture challenges us to do so. Paul says in 2 Corinthians 13:5, "Examine yourselves to see whether you are in the faith." In 2 Peter 1:10, we're told to "be all the more eager to make your calling and election sure." Test yourself to see if you have eternal life. Determine if you have the fruit of the Spirit. That's how you can know. Now that we have unpacked the first truth—we can know we have salvation because God's word says so—let's move on to the second reason why we have assurance.

Facts, Faith, Fruit

The second way we know we are saved is to focus on facts, faith, and fruit. Let's start with the facts. The fact is, "Christ died for our sins according to the Scriptures, that he was buried, that he was raised on the third day" (1 Cor. 15:3–4). Now, let's look at faith. Faith is the conviction that divine action makes us Christians and nothing else. "He who has the Son has life; he who does not have the Son of God does not have life (1 John 5:12). It is that simple. Then, as explained earlier, there will be fruit. Jesus said we can recognize other Christians "by their fruit" (Matt. 7:16, 20). Given time, faith will produce the fruit of the Spirit. Facts, faith, and fruit—these three are essential to providing assurance of salvation.

Saved by Grace, Kept by the Grip of God

Finally, our assurance depends on the belief that we are saved by God's grace and kept by his grip. The Scriptures say, "For it is by grace you have been saved, through faith—and this not from yourselves, it is the gift of God—not by works, so that no one can boast" (Ephesians 2:8–9). Grace is unmerited favor. It speaks of something we need (salvation) and do not deserve, that God freely gives.

Then we are also kept by the grip of God. Fritz von Erick's family became the most popular wrestlers in the world years ago. When I first met him, he lived in Edom, Texas, a small town near where I live in Tyler. He occasionally visited our church, and I in turn visited him and his wife in their home. I even asked him to join me one time in an evangelistic crusade to share his testimony.

Fritz was like a modern day Job. His life was filled with tragedy. He and his wife had six boys, and five of them died tragically. One of them died from an unexplained illness, two of them died from drug overdoses, one committed suicide, and one died in an automobile accident. The strain of losing all their sons except for one was more than their marriage could stand, and finally he and his wife of many years separated.

Fritz then moved from Edom to Lewisville, Texas, and was living there alone the last time we visited together. He soon learned that he had cancer. When he was at the point of death, he began having doubts about his salvation. His one remaining son asked Boone Powell, administrator of Baylor Hospital in Dallas, to visit with him. Fritz was a gentle giant with huge hands. Among other things, he was famous for gripping his opponent's forehead in a move called the Iron Claw. Supposedly, when he got a fellow wrestler in that grip he could not escape.

As Boone tried to give him assurance of his salvation he asked, "Fritz, what was that grip you used to use on other wrestlers?"

Fritz replied, "The Iron Claw."

"When you got people in that grip, could they get away?"

Fritz shook his head and said, "In no way."

Then Boone explained, "Fritz, that's what Jesus has got on you. He's got you and you can't get away."

George Beverly Shea once told his audience that one of the occupational hazards of being a well-known gospel singer is that people often sent him original songs they wanted him to sing. One songwriter sent him a composition entitled, "God's Grip Doesn't Slip!" It was not much of a song, but what a title. There's affirmation in Scripture for that. Jesus said,

> My sheep listen to my voice; I know them, and they follow me. I give them eternal life, and they shall never perish; no one can snatch them out of my hand. My Father, who has given them to me, is greater than all; no one can snatch them out of my Father's hand (John 10:27–29).

Saved by the grace of God, kept in the grip of God. That's the grounds and guarantee of our salvation. And, Christian friend, you cost Christ too much for him to let go.

Assurance of salvation is one of God's beautiful gifts to us. We don't have to live in the fog of doubt. We can know for certain that we are going to heaven. Here is the clincher.

> That if you confess with your mouth, "Jesus is Lord," and believe in your heart that God raised him from the dead, you will be saved. For it is with your heart that you believe and are justified, and it is with your mouth that you confess and are saved. As the Scripture says, "Anyone who trusts in him will never be put to shame" (Rom. 10:9–11).

Are you saved? Your answer cannot be, "I think so." Not, "I hope so." Your answer should be, "I know so!" "Everyone who calls on the name of the Lord will be saved" (Rom. 10:13). That ought to be assurance enough for anyone.

At the time of this writing, Billy Graham is in his nineties and living with Parkinson's disease. Several years ago, a group of leaders in Charlotte, North Carolina, invited their favorite son to a luncheon in his honor. Graham initially hesitated to accept because of his health. But the Charlotte leaders assured him they just wanted him to come so they could honor him, and he agreed to attend.

After hearing the wonderful things said about him, Graham stepped to the podium and told a funny story about Albert Einstein. Einstein was once traveling by train from Princeton when the conductor came down the aisle, punching the tickets of every passenger. When he came to Einstein, Einstein reached in his vest pocket. He couldn't find his ticket, so he reached in his trouser pockets. It wasn't there. He looked in his briefcase and in the seat beside him to no avail.

The conductor smiled and said, "Dr. Einstein, I know who you are. We all know who you are. I'm sure you bought a ticket. Don't worry about it."

Einstein nodded appreciatively as the conductor continued down the aisle. Before moving to the next car, the conductor turned around to see the great physicist down on his hands and knees still looking under his seat for his ticket. The conductor rushed back and assured him not to worry. "Dr. Einstein," he told him, "I know who you are. No problem."

Einstein looked at him and said, "Young man, I too know who I am. What I don't know is where I'm going."

After the laughter died down, Billy Graham explained that he was wearing a new suit for the luncheon, joking that his children and grandchildren had told him he'd grown a little slovenly in his old age. He told them he bought the suit for that day and one more occasion. "You know what that occasion is?" he asked. "This is the suit in which I'll be buried. But when you hear I'm dead, I don't want you to immediately remember the suit I'm wearing. I want you to remember this: I not only know who I am, but I also know where I'm going."

Do you know where you are going? I hope so. And I hope it's to heaven.

Conclusion

Time is passing us by. What will you do with what you have left? I saved the final two chapters for the end because when we die—or when Jesus returns—time as we know it will be no more. One day it will be too late to make the most of our days because the last leaf will have fallen.

Today is a good day to start living the rest of your life for Christ. Sometimes people put off making important changes in their priorities because they think they have all the time in the world to do so. However, time is always shorter than we think. We must decide today to trust Jesus and fully commit to honoring him because tomorrow is uncertain for everyone.

In this book, I've suggested several practical starting points for you to live each day with a greater sense of purpose so that when you come to the end of your life you will be sure you've given Christ your all. If you recall, you can watch your money, or work on your tendency to worry, or make a stronger commitment to being in church. You can also be a better neighbor—regardless of the cost—and learn to hang on to Jesus whenever you are going through tough times. There are many other ways to grow in the Christian life and start making a greater impact for Christ. However, the most important thing is that you start somewhere.

I suggest you pick one of these twelve chapters, read through it again, and start putting it into practice this week. At the end of twelve weeks, you will have grown in your relationship with Christ and made progress in a dozen ways toward living with greater purpose. Whatever you do, don't come to the end of your life with regrets. Instead, invest your time wisely now by knowing and applying what Jesus teaches about what it means to live for him in every season of life.

I heard a story about James Brit Bailey, one of the early colonists in Texas. Bailey was born in North Carolina in 1779, but he moved to Texas around 1818 and settled near the Brazos River in an area that is known today as Bailey's Prairie. Bailey was quite a character. Having fought in the War of 1812 and other subsequent battles, he was known as a quick-tempered brawler who was also very eccentric. One of his most famous eccentricities was the unusual request in his will to be buried in the family graveyard standing straight up, facing the setting sun![1]

When the last leaf falls, I want to be remembered as standing for something, don't you? Like Bailey, I have always said I want to go down standing up—standing up for truth and for righteousness. And I want to die facing the future with hope and optimism. That being said, I would also like to be remembered as bowing to at least one man—the Lord

Jesus. To fail to "stoop" to him is to fail in life in the highest sense, no matter how you stand or which way you face.

If you apply the basics of what the Bible teaches about a life well lived, you can be sure that you are redeeming the time. The Bible says God "works in you to will and to act according to his good purpose" (Philippians 2:13) When you put your faith in Jesus, he can enable you to make the most of life—one day at a time.

NOTES

1. https://tshaonline.org/handbook/online/articles/umo01. Accessed 2/8/16.